Based on the Texas Essential Knowledge and Skills (TEKS)

# STAAR

# SUCCESS STRATEGIES
# Grade 6
# Mathematics

STAAR Test Review for the State of
Texas Assessments of Academic Readiness

Dear Future Exam Success Story:

First of all, **THANK YOU** for purchasing Mometrix study materials!

Second, congratulations! You are one of the few determined test-takers who are committed to doing whatever it takes to excel on your exam. **You have come to the right place.** We developed these study materials with one goal in mind: to deliver you the information you need in a format that's concise and easy to use.

In addition to optimizing your guide for the content of the test, we've outlined our recommended steps for breaking down the preparation process into small, attainable goals so you can make sure you stay on track.

We've also analyzed the entire test-taking process, identifying the most common pitfalls and showing how you can overcome them and be ready for any curveball the test throws you.

Standardized testing is one of the biggest obstacles on your road to success, which only increases the importance of doing well in the high-pressure, high-stakes environment of test day. Your results on this test could have a significant impact on your future, and this guide provides the information and practical advice to help you achieve your full potential on test day.

**Your success is our success**

**We would love to hear from you!** If you would like to share the story of your exam success or if you have any questions or comments in regard to our products, please contact us at **800-673-8175** or **support@mometrix.com**.

Thanks again for your business and we wish you continued success!

Sincerely,
The Mometrix Test Preparation Team

**Need more help? Check out our flashcards at:** http://MometrixFlashcards.com/STAAR

# TABLE OF CONTENTS

# Introduction

**Thank you for purchasing this resource**! You have made the choice to prepare yourself for a test that could have a huge impact on your future, and this guide is designed to help you be fully ready for test day. Obviously, it's important to have a solid understanding of the test material, but you also need to be prepared for the unique environment and stressors of the test, so that you can perform to the best of your abilities.

For this purpose, the first section that appears in this guide is the **Success Strategies**. We've devoted countless hours to meticulously researching what works and what doesn't, and we've boiled down our findings to the five most impactful steps you can take to improve your performance on the test. We start at the beginning with study planning and move through the preparation process, all the way to the testing strategies that will help you get the most out of what you know when you're finally sitting in front of the test.

We recommend that you start preparing for your test as far in advance as possible. However, if you've bought this guide as a last-minute study resource and only have a few days before your test, we recommend that you skip over the first two Success Strategies since they address a long-term study plan.

If you struggle with **test anxiety**, we strongly encourage you to check out our recommendations for how you can overcome it. Test anxiety is a formidable foe, but it can be beaten, and we want to make sure you have the tools you need to defeat it.

# Success Strategy #1 – Plan Big, Study Small

There's a lot riding on your performance. If you want to ace this test, you're going to need to keep your skills sharp and the material fresh in your mind. You need a plan that lets you review everything you need to know while still fitting in your schedule. We'll break this strategy down into three categories.

## Information Organization

Start with the information you already have: the official test outline. From this, you can make a complete list of all the concepts you need to cover before the test. Organize these concepts into groups that can be studied together, and create a list of any related vocabulary you need to learn so you can brush up on any difficult terms. You'll want to keep this vocabulary list handy once you actually start studying since you may need to add to it along the way.

## Time Management

Once you have your set of study concepts, decide how to spread them out over the time you have left before the test. Break your study plan into small, clear goals so you have a manageable task for each day and know exactly what you're doing. Then just focus on one small step at a time. When you manage your time this way, you don't need to spend hours at a time studying. Studying a small block of content for a short period each day helps you retain information better and avoid stressing over how much you have left to do. You can relax knowing that you have a plan to cover everything in time. In order for this strategy to be effective though, you have to start studying early and stick to your schedule. Avoid the exhaustion and futility that comes from last-minute cramming!

## Study Environment

The environment you study in has a big impact on your learning. Studying in a coffee shop, while probably more enjoyable, is not likely to be as fruitful as studying in a quiet room. It's important to keep distractions to a minimum. You're only planning to study for a short block of time, so make the most of it. Don't pause to check your phone or get up to find a snack. It's also important to **avoid multitasking**. Research has consistently shown that multitasking will make your studying dramatically less effective. Your study area should also be comfortable and well-lit so you don't have the distraction of straining your eyes or sitting on an uncomfortable chair.

The time of day you study is also important. You want to be rested and alert. Don't wait until just before bedtime. Study when you'll be most likely to comprehend and remember. Even better, if you know what time of day your test will be, set that time aside for study. That way your brain will be used to working on that subject at that specific time and you'll have a better chance of recalling information.

Finally, it can be helpful to team up with others who are studying for the same test. Your actual studying should be done in as isolated an environment as possible, but the work of organizing the information and setting up the study plan can be divided up. In between study sessions, you can discuss with your teammates the concepts that you're all studying and quiz each other on the details. Just be sure that your teammates are as serious about the test as you are. If you find that your study time is being replaced with social time, you might need to find a new team.

# Success Strategy #2 – Make Your Studying Count

You're devoting a lot of time and effort to preparing for this test, so you want to be absolutely certain it will pay off. This means doing more than just reading the content and hoping you can remember it on test day. It's important to make every minute of study count. There are two main areas you can focus on to make your studying count:

## Retention

It doesn't matter how much time you study if you can't remember the material. You need to make sure you are retaining the concepts. To check your retention of the information you're learning, try recalling it at later times with minimal prompting. Try carrying around flashcards and glance at one or two from time to time or ask a friend who's also studying for the test to quiz you.

To enhance your retention, look for ways to put the information into practice so that you can apply it rather than simply recalling it. If you're using the information in practical ways, it will be much easier to remember. Similarly, it helps to solidify a concept in your mind if you're not only reading it to yourself but also explaining it to someone else. Ask a friend to let you teach them about a concept you're a little shaky on (or speak aloud to an imaginary audience if necessary). As you try to summarize, define, give examples, and answer your friend's questions, you'll understand the concepts better and they will stay with you longer. Finally, step back for a big picture view and ask yourself how each piece of information fits with the whole subject. When you link the different concepts together and see them working together as a whole, it's easier to remember the individual components.

Finally, practice showing your work on any multi-step problems, even if you're just studying. Writing out each step you take to solve a problem will help solidify the process in your mind, and you'll be more likely to remember it during the test.

## Modality

*Modality* simply refers to the means or method by which you study. Choosing a study modality that fits your own individual learning style is crucial. No two people learn best in exactly the same way, so it's important to know your strengths and use them to your advantage.

For example, if you learn best by visualization, focus on visualizing a concept in your mind and draw an image or a diagram. Try color-coding your notes, illustrating them, or creating symbols that will trigger your mind to recall a learned concept. If you learn best by hearing or discussing information, find a study partner who learns the same way or read aloud to yourself. Think about how to put the information in your own words. Imagine that you are giving a lecture on the topic and record yourself so you can listen to it later.

For any learning style, flashcards can be helpful. Organize the information so you can take advantage of spare moments to review. Underline key words or phrases. Use different colors for different categories. Mnemonic devices (such as creating a short list in which every item starts with the same letter) can also help with retention. Find what works best for you and use it to store the information in your mind most effectively and easily.

# Success Strategy #3 – Practice the Right Way

Your success on test day depends not only on how many hours you put into preparing, but also on whether you prepared the right way. It's good to check along the way to see if your studying is paying off. One of the most effective ways to do this is by taking practice tests to evaluate your progress. Practice tests are useful because they show exactly where you need to improve. Every time you take a practice test, pay special attention to these three groups of questions:

- The questions you got wrong
- The questions you had to guess on, even if you guessed right
- The questions you found difficult or slow to work through

This will show you exactly what your weak areas are, and where you need to devote more study time. Ask yourself why each of these questions gave you trouble. Was it because you didn't understand the material? Was it because you didn't remember the vocabulary? Do you need more repetitions on this type of question to build speed and confidence? Dig into those questions and figure out how you can strengthen your weak areas as you go back to review the material.

Additionally, many practice tests have a section explaining the answer choices. It can be tempting to read the explanation and think that you now have a good understanding of the concept. However, an explanation likely only covers part of the question's broader context. Even if the explanation makes sense, **go back and investigate** every concept related to the question until you're positive you have a thorough understanding.

As you go along, keep in mind that the practice test is just that: practice. Memorizing these questions and answers will not be very helpful on the actual test because it is unlikely to have any of the same exact questions. If you only know the right answers to the sample questions, you won't be prepared for the real thing. **Study the concepts** until you understand them fully, and then you'll be able to answer any question that shows up on the test.

It's important to wait on the practice tests until you're ready. If you take a test on your first day of study, you may be overwhelmed by the amount of material covered and how much you need to learn. Work up to it gradually.

On test day, you'll need to be prepared for answering questions, managing your time, and using the test-taking strategies you've learned. It's a lot to balance, like a mental marathon that will have a big impact on your future. Like training for a marathon, you'll need to start slowly and work your way up. When test day arrives, you'll be ready.

Start with what you've read in the first two Success Strategies—plan your course and study in the way that works best for you. If you have time, consider using multiple study resources to get different approaches to the same concepts. It can be helpful to see difficult concepts from more than one angle. Then find a good source for practice tests. Many times, the test website will suggest potential study resources or provide sample tests.

# Practice Test Strategy

When you're ready to start taking practice tests, follow this strategy:

## Untimed and Open-Book Practice

Take the first test with no time constraints and with your notes and study guide handy. Take your time and focus on applying the strategies you've learned.

## Timed and Open-Book Practice

Take the second practice test open-book as well, but set a timer and practice pacing yourself to finish in time.

## Timed and Closed-Book Practice

Take any other practice tests as if it were test day. Set a timer and put away your study materials. Sit at a table or desk in a quiet room, imagine yourself at the testing center, and answer questions as quickly and accurately as possible.

Keep repeating timed and closed-book tests on a regular basis until you run out of practice tests or it's time for the actual test. Your mind will be ready for the schedule and stress of test day, and you'll be able to focus on recalling the material you've learned.

# Success Strategy #4 – Pace Yourself

Once you're fully prepared for the material on the test, your biggest challenge on test day will be managing your time. Just knowing that the clock is ticking can make you panic even if you have plenty of time left. Work on pacing yourself so you can build confidence against the time constraints of the exam. Pacing is a difficult skill to master, especially in a high-pressure environment, so **practice is vital**.

Set time expectations for your pace based on how much time is available. For example, if a section has 60 questions and the time limit is 30 minutes, you know you have to average 30 seconds or less per question in order to answer them all. Although 30 seconds is the hard limit, set 25 seconds per question as your goal, so you reserve extra time to spend on harder questions. When you budget extra time for the harder questions, you no longer have any reason to stress when those questions take longer to answer.

Don't let this time expectation distract you from working through the test at a calm, steady pace, but keep it in mind so you don't spend too much time on any one question. Recognize that taking extra time on one question you don't understand may keep you from answering two that you do understand later in the test. If your time limit for a question is up and you're still not sure of the answer, mark it and move on, and come back to it later if the time and the test format allow. If the testing format doesn't allow you to return to earlier questions, just make an educated guess; then put it out of your mind and move on.

On the easier questions, be careful not to rush. It may seem wise to hurry through them so you have more time for the challenging ones, but it's not worth missing one if you know the concept and just didn't take the time to read the question fully. Work efficiently but make sure you understand the question and have looked at all of the answer choices, since more than one may seem right at first.

Even if you're paying attention to the time, you may find yourself a little behind at some point. You should speed up to get back on track, but do so wisely. Don't panic; just take a few seconds less on each question until you're caught up. Don't guess without thinking, but do look through the answer choices and eliminate any you know are wrong. If you can get down to two choices, it is often worthwhile to guess from those. Once you've chosen an answer, move on and don't dwell on any that you skipped or had to hurry through. If a question was taking too long, chances are it was one of the harder ones, so you weren't as likely to get it right anyway.

On the other hand, if you find yourself getting ahead of schedule, it may be beneficial to slow down a little. The more quickly you work, the more likely you are to make a careless mistake that will affect your score. You've budgeted time for each question, so don't be afraid to spend that time. Practice an efficient but careful pace to get the most out of the time you have.

# Test-Taking Strategies

This section contains a list of test-taking strategies that you may find helpful as you work through the test. By taking what you know and applying logical thought, you can maximize your chances of answering any question correctly!

It is very important to realize that every question is different and every person is different: no single strategy will work on every question, and no single strategy will work for every person. That's why we've included all of them here, so you can try them out and determine which ones work best for different types of questions and which ones work best for you.

## Question Strategies

### Read Carefully

Read the question and answer choices carefully. Don't miss the question because you misread the terms. You have plenty of time to read each question thoroughly and make sure you understand what is being asked. Yet a happy medium must be attained, so don't waste too much time. You must read carefully, but efficiently.

### Contextual Clues

Look for contextual clues. If the question includes a word you are not familiar with, look at the immediate context for some indication of what the word might mean. Contextual clues can often give you all the information you need to decipher the meaning of an unfamiliar word. Even if you can't determine the meaning, you may be able to narrow down the possibilities enough to make a solid guess at the answer to the question.

### Prefixes

If you're having trouble with a word in the question or answer choices, try dissecting it. Take advantage of every clue that the word might include. Prefixes and suffixes can be a huge help. Usually they allow you to determine a basic meaning. Pre- means before, post- means after, pro - is positive, de- is negative. From prefixes and suffixes, you can get an idea of the general meaning of the word and try to put it into context.

### Hedge Words

Watch out for critical hedge words, such as *likely, may, can, sometimes, often, almost, mostly, usually, generally, rarely,* and *sometimes.* Question writers insert these hedge phrases to cover every possibility. Often an answer choice will be wrong simply because it leaves no room for exception. Be on guard for answer choices that have definitive words such as *exactly* and *always.*

### Switchback Words

Stay alert for *switchbacks.* These are the words and phrases frequently used to alert you to shifts in thought. The most common switchback words are *but, although,* and *however.* Others include *nevertheless, on the other hand, even though, while, in spite of, despite, regardless of.* Switchback words are important to catch because they can change the direction of the question or an answer choice.

## Face Value

When in doubt, use common sense. Accept the situation in the problem at face value. Don't read too much into it. These problems will not require you to make wild assumptions. If you have to go beyond creativity and warp time or space in order to have an answer choice fit the question, then you should move on and consider the other answer choices. These are normal problems rooted in reality. The applicable relationship or explanation may not be readily apparent, but it is there for you to figure out. Use your common sense to interpret anything that isn't clear.

# Answer Choice Strategies

## Answer Selection

The most thorough way to pick an answer choice is to identify and eliminate wrong answers until only one is left, then confirm it is the correct answer. Sometimes an answer choice may immediately seem right, but be careful. The test writers will usually put more than one reasonable answer choice on each question, so take a second to read all of them and make sure that the other choices are not equally obvious. As long as you have time left, it is better to read every answer choice than to pick the first one that looks right without checking the others.

## Answer Choice Families

An answer choice family consists of two (in rare cases, three) answer choices that are very similar in construction and cannot all be true at the same time. If you see two answer choices that are direct opposites or parallels, one of them is usually the correct answer. For instance, if one answer choice says that quantity $x$ increases and another either says that quantity $x$ decreases (opposite) or says that quantity $y$ increases (parallel), then those answer choices would fall into the same family. An answer choice that doesn't match the construction of the answer choice family is more likely to be incorrect. Most questions will not have answer choice families, but when they do appear, you should be prepared to recognize them.

## Eliminate Answers

Eliminate answer choices as soon as you realize they are wrong, but make sure you consider all possibilities. If you are eliminating answer choices and realize that the last one you are left with is also wrong, don't panic. Start over and consider each choice again. There may be something you missed the first time that you will realize on the second pass.

## Avoid Fact Traps

Don't be distracted by an answer choice that is factually true but doesn't answer the question. You are looking for the choice that answers the question. Stay focused on what the question is asking for so you don't accidentally pick an answer that is true but incorrect. Always go back to the question and make sure the answer choice you've selected actually answers the question and is not merely a true statement.

## Extreme Statements

In general, you should avoid answers that put forth extreme actions as standard practice or proclaim controversial ideas as established fact. An answer choice that states the "process should be used in certain situations, if…" is much more likely to be correct than one that states the "process should be discontinued completely." The first is a calm rational statement and doesn't even make a definitive, uncompromising stance, using a hedge word *if* to provide wiggle room, whereas the second choice is a radical idea and far more extreme.

### Benchmark

As you read through the answer choices and you come across one that seems to answer the question well, mentally select that answer choice. This is not your final answer, but it's the one that will help you evaluate the other answer choices. The one that you selected is your benchmark or standard for judging each of the other answer choices. Every other answer choice must be compared to your benchmark. That choice is correct until proven otherwise by another answer choice beating it. If you find a better answer, then that one becomes your new benchmark. Once you've decided that no other choice answers the question as well as your benchmark, you have your final answer.

### Predict the Answer

Before you even start looking at the answer choices, it is often best to try to predict the answer. When you come up with the answer on your own, it is easier to avoid distractions and traps because you will know exactly what to look for. The right answer choice is unlikely to be word-for-word what you came up with, but it should be a close match. Even if you are confident that you have the right answer, you should still take the time to read each option before moving on.

# General Strategies

### Tough Questions

If you are stumped on a problem or it appears too hard or too difficult, don't waste time. Move on! Remember though, if you can quickly check for obviously incorrect answer choices, your chances of guessing correctly are greatly improved. Before you completely give up, at least try to knock out a couple of possible answers. Eliminate what you can and then guess at the remaining answer choices before moving on.

### Check Your Work

Since you will probably not know every term listed and the answer to every question, it is important that you get credit for the ones that you do know. Don't miss any questions through careless mistakes. If at all possible, try to take a second to look back over your answer selection and make sure you've selected the correct answer choice and haven't made a costly careless mistake (such as marking an answer choice that you didn't mean to mark). This quick double check should more than pay for itself in caught mistakes for the time it costs.

### Pace Yourself

It's easy to be overwhelmed when you're looking at a page full of questions; your mind is confused and full of random thoughts, and the clock is ticking down faster than you would like. Calm down and maintain the pace that you have set for yourself. Especially as you get down to the last few minutes of the test, don't let the small numbers on the clock make you panic. As long as you are on track by monitoring your pace, you are guaranteed to have time for each question.

## Don't Rush

It is very easy to make errors when you are in a hurry. Maintaining a fast pace in answering questions is pointless if it makes you miss questions that you would have gotten right otherwise. Test writers like to include distracting information and wrong answers that seem right. Taking a little extra time to avoid careless mistakes can make all the difference in your test score. Find a pace that allows you to be confident in the answers that you select.

## Keep Moving

Panicking will not help you pass the test, so do your best to stay calm and keep moving. Taking deep breaths and going through the answer elimination steps you practiced can help to break through a stress barrier and keep your pace.

# Final Notes

The combination of a solid foundation of content knowledge and the confidence that comes from practicing your plan for applying that knowledge is the key to maximizing your performance on test day. As your foundation of content knowledge is built up and strengthened, you'll find that the strategies included in this chapter become more and more effective in helping you quickly sift through the distractions and traps of the test to isolate the correct answer.

Now it's time to move on to the test content chapters of this book, but be sure to keep your goal in mind. As you read, think about how you will be able to apply this information on the test. If you've already seen sample questions for the test and you have an idea of the question format and style, try to come up with questions of your own that you can answer based on what you're reading. This will give you valuable practice applying your knowledge in the same ways you can expect to on test day.

**Good luck and good studying!**

# Numerical Representations and Relationships

## Integer, Percent, Fraction, and Decimal

An integer is a positive whole number, negative whole number, or zero; for example, 8 is an integer. A percent is a part per hundred; for example, 20% is 20 parts per hundred. A fraction is an expression where one number is being divided by another; for example, $\frac{20}{10}$ is a fraction. All rational numbers can be written as a positive or negative whole number, or zero, being divided by another positive or negative whole number. A decimal contains a whole number (or zero), which is to the left of the decimal point, and a portion of a whole number, which is to the right of the decimal point; for example, 20.53 is a number is decimal form. All rational numbers are either terminating decimals, where the numbers to the right of the decimal point end, or repeating decimals, where the numbers to the right of the decimal repeat in a pattern infinitely. Integers, percents, fractions, and decimals are all forms of rational numbers.

## Rational Numbers from Least to Greatest

### Example

Order the following rational numbers from least to greatest: 12%, 1.2, $\frac{1}{12}$, 12.

> The first step to solve this is to convert all of the rational numbers in to a common form. For this example we will use decimal form. The 12% as a decimal would be 0.12, and the $\frac{1}{12}$ as a decimal would be ~0.083. The 1.2 and 12 are already in this form. The next step is to then arrange them from least to greatest, which is .083, .12, 1.2, and 12. After they are arranged in the correct order they can be converted back to the original form. So the final answer would be:
>
> From least to greatest: $\frac{1}{12}$, 12%, 1.2, 12.

## Equivalent Forms of Rational Numbers

As discussed above rational numbers can come in several forms. It will be important to be able to convert rational numbers between forms.

### Example 1

Convert each quantity below. Identify the form of each given quantity and describe the new form of the quantity.

> a) Write 0.25 as a fraction.
> b) Write 0.4 as a percent.

a) 0.25 is a decimal number. A fraction is an expression where one number is being divided by another. To write a decimal number as a fraction, count the number of places right of the decimal. Write a 1 followed by as many zeros as there are decimal places. The fraction will be the decimal number written without a decimal point divided by the number written in the previous step. The fraction can then be reduced by dividing the top and bottom by the same number.

$$0.25 = \frac{25}{100} = \frac{1}{4}$$

b) 0.4 is a decimal. A percent is a part per hundred. To write a decimal as a percent, move the decimal place two digits to the right.

0.4 = 40%

<u>Example 2</u>

Convert each quantity below. Identify the form of each given quantity and describe the new form of the quantity.

    a) Write $\frac{3}{4}$ as a decimal.
    b) Write 200% as a whole number.
    a) $\frac{3}{4}$ is a fraction. A decimal contains a whole number (or zero), which is to the left of the decimal point, and a portion of a whole number, which is to the right of the decimal point. In this case there is no whole number so our decimal would be 0.75.
    b) 200% is a percent. A whole number is a positive integer or zero. To write a percent as a whole number, first write the percent as a decimal. Move the decimal two places to the left.

$$200\% = 2.00$$

If the quantity after the decimal is 0, then the number can be written as a whole number by only writing the whole number portion of the decimal.

$$2.00 = 2$$

Venn diagram

A Venn diagram uses circles to show the intersection of sets. The example below shows the numbers that are divisible by 2 and 3 between 1 and 20, and the numbers divisible by both in the intersection.

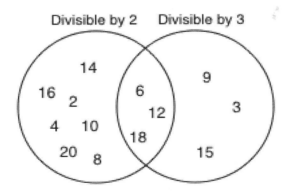

**Absolute value**

Absolute Value is how far away a number is from zero on a number line, or the distance between zero and that number. The absolute value of a number is always positive, because distance is positive.

The absolute value of 40 is 40, because it is 40 units away from zero.
The absolute value of -12 is 12 because it is 12 units away from zero.
The absolute value of -25 is 25 because it is 25 units away from zero.

- 13 -

The absolute value of 18 is 18 because it is 18 units away from zero.
The absolute value of -100 is 100 because it is 100 units away from zero.

## Equivalent Ratios

A ratio is used to describe how two or more quantities are related. An equivalent ratio can be found by multiplying or dividing both sides by the same number. For example 2:6 is equivalent to 4:12. Both sides were multiplied by two.

Example 1

A supermarket advertises a special price of $3.00 for 5 oranges. The regular price is $2.50 for 4 oranges. Compare the unit prices of sale and regular-priced oranges.

> To find the unit price of sale and regular-priced oranges, find the price of one orange, or the price per orange. The price of a single orange can be found by dividing the total price by the total number of oranges. The price should be rounded to the nearest cent, or hundredth, since this is the smallest unit of dollars.

Sale price: $\frac{\$3.00}{5 \text{ oranges}} = \frac{\$0.60}{1 \text{ orange}}$

Regular price $\frac{\$2.50}{4 \text{ oranges}} = \frac{\$0.63}{1 \text{ orange}}$:

The sale price is: $0.63 – $0.60 = $0.03 less than the regular price.

Example 2

T-shirts are sold in packages of multiple shirts. Three t-shirts are sold in one package for $8.00. Five t-shirts are sold in a second package for $12.00. Compare the price of a single t-shirt from the two packages.

> To find the price of each t-shirt, divide the quantity of shirts in each package by the cost of each package. The cost of each shirt should be rounded to the nearest cent, or hundredth, since this is the smallest unit of dollars.

Package 1: $\frac{\$8.00}{3} = \$2.67$

Package 2: $\frac{\$12.00}{5} = \$2.40$

> The price per t-shirt is cheaper if purchasing the five t-shirts for $12.00.

## Percentage

One *Percent* means one part per hundred, so a percentage is the ratio of a number to 100. For example, 42% can be written as the ratio $\frac{42}{100}$ or its reduced equivalent, $\frac{21}{50}$.

Example

> Write each percentage as a simplified fraction and as a decimal:

- 32%
- 135%

> A percentage is a ratio of a number to 100.

$$32\% = \frac{32}{100} = \frac{8}{25} \ or \ \frac{32}{100} = 0.32$$
$$135\% = \frac{135}{100} = 1\frac{35}{100} = 1\frac{7}{20}$$
$$\frac{135}{100} = 1\frac{35}{100} = 1.35$$

## Example

Write each number as a percentage

$$\frac{4}{5}$$
$$\frac{2}{3}$$

$$0.23 = \frac{23}{100} = 23\%$$
$$\frac{4}{5} = \frac{80}{100} = 80\%$$
$$\frac{2}{3} = 0.\overline{6} = 66.\overline{6}\%$$

## Example

Express the shaded portion of the circle as a fraction, a decimal, and a percentage.

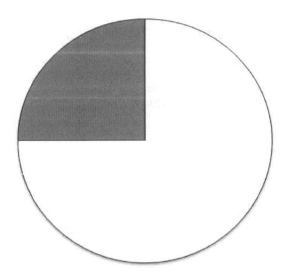

¼ of the circle's area is shaded. $\frac{1}{4} = 0.25 = \frac{25}{100} = 25\%$.

## Using proportions to solve percent problems

A proportion is a statement of equivalence between two ratios. In percent problems, both ratios compare parts to a whole; in particular, a percentage expresses parts per 100. A proportion which can be used to solved a percent problem is $\frac{part}{whole} = \frac{percent}{100}$.

In the given scenario, 4 is 80% of some number $a$, so 4 represents part of the unknown number. The proportion, therefore, is $\frac{4}{a} = \frac{80}{100}$. There are many ways to solve proportions. Notice that $\frac{80}{100}$ reduces to $\frac{4}{5}$, so $a = 5$.

## Example 1

A family of six dines at a restaurant which charges an automatic gratuity for parties of six or more. A tip of $28 is added to their bill of $80. Determine the percent gratuity charged.

One way to determine the percent gratuity charged is to set up and solve a proportion of the form

$$\frac{part}{whole} = \frac{percent}{100}.$$

$$\frac{28}{80} = \frac{p}{100}$$

There are many ways to solve proportions. Notice that $\frac{28}{80}$ reduces to $\frac{7}{20}$, which can easily be converted to a fraction with a denominator of 100 by multiplying the numerator and denominator by 5.

$$\frac{7 \times 5}{20 \times 5} = \frac{35}{100}$$

So, $p = 35$. The gratuity added is 35%.

## Example 2

The ratio of flour to sugar in a cookie recipe is 3:1. Find the amount of sugar needed for 1 ½ cups of flour

There are many ways to solve this problem using proportional reasoning. One way is to notice that the amount of flour divided by three gives the amount of sugar.

cups of flour: cups of sugar

$$\overset{\div 3}{\frown}\\ 3{:}1$$

So, the amount of sugar needed for 1 ½ cups of flour can be found by dividing $1\frac{1}{2}$ by 3. $1\frac{1}{2} \div 3 = \frac{3}{2} \times \frac{1}{3} = \frac{3}{6} = \frac{1}{2}$.

$$\overset{\div 3}{\frown}\\ 1\frac{1}{2}{:}\frac{1}{2}$$

The amount of sugar needed is ½ cup.

- 16 -

<u>Example 3</u>

Suppose you purchase a $7.00 entrée and a $2.00 drink at your favorite restaurant.

- Determine the amount of a 10% tax on your purchase.
- Determine the amount of a 15% tip on the pre-tax amount.
- Find the total price of the meal, including tax and tip.

The amount of your purchase before tax and tip is $9.00. There are many way to calculate the amount of tax on the purchase. One method is to set up and solve a proportion:

The amount of the tax will be calculated as a fraction of the purchase price. That fraction comparing the tax amount to the pre-tax price is equal to 10%, or $\frac{10}{100}$. So, $\frac{tax\ amount}{\$9.00} = \frac{10}{100}$. A tax amount of $0.90 satisfies the proportion.

Another method involves translating the problem into a mathematical expression which represents the tax amount, which is *10% of the purchase.*

A percent is a ratio out of 100, so $10\% = \frac{10}{100} = 0.10$.

The word "of" indicates multiplication.

The purchase price is $9.

So, *10% of the purchase* translates to $0.10 \times \$9$, which equals $0.90.

Again, there are many ways to calculate the amount of the tip. 15% of $9.00 translates to $0.15 \times \$9$, which equals $1.35.

The total price is the cost of the meal plus the tax plus the tip: $9.00+$0.90+$1.35=$11.25.

## Diagram and Equation to Represent a Fraction

A pie chart can be used to represent fractions. The chart is divided into equal sections based on the denominator of the fraction. Then the numerator of the fraction can be expressed by shading the number of equivalent sections.

<u>Example</u>

A pie is divided into 8 equal pieces. There are 5 pieces remaining. Draw a picture to determine what fraction of the pie is remaining if 2 additional pieces are eaten. Then write an equation represented by the diagram.

Draw a circle, and divide the circle into 8 equal pieces. Then shade 5 of the pieces to show the pieces remaining.

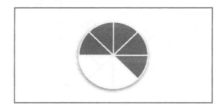

From the pieces remaining, two pieces are eaten. This can be symbolized by shading these two pieces differently.

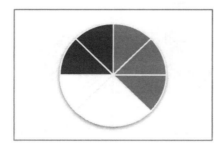

There are 3 of the original 8 pieces remaining, which is $\frac{3}{8}$ of the pie. This can be expressed with the equation: $\frac{5}{8} - \frac{2}{8} = \frac{3}{8}$.

## Addition and Subtraction of Fractions and Decimals

Fractions and decimals can be added and subtracted just like whole numbers. To add or subtract fractions and decimals, first make sure that the numbers are in the same form. The answer can be written as either a fraction or decimal. If using fractions, the fractions must have a common denominator.

<u>Example</u>

Solve these equations: a) $7.1 - \frac{3}{4}$; b) $\frac{6}{5} + 0.4$

a)

$$7.1 - \frac{3}{4} = \frac{71}{10} - \frac{3}{4} = \frac{142}{20} - \frac{15}{20} = \frac{127}{20}$$

b)

$$\frac{6}{5} + 0.4 = \frac{6}{5} + \frac{2}{5} = \frac{8}{5} = 1.6$$

- 18 -

## Order of Operations

Order of Operations is a set of rules that dictates the order in which we must perform each operation in an expression so that we will evaluate it accurately. If we have an expression that includes multiple different operations, Order of Operations tells us which operations to do first. The most common mnemonic for Order of Operations is PEMDAS, or "Please Excuse My Dear Aunt Sally." PEMDAS stands for Parentheses, Exponents, Multiplication, Division, Addition, and Subtraction. It is important to understand that multiplication and division have equal precedence, as do addition and subtraction, so those pairs of operations are simply worked from left to right in order.

### Example 1

Evaluate the expression $5 + 20 \div 4 \times (2 + 3)^2 - 6$ using the correct order of operations.

P: Perform the operations inside the parentheses, $(2 + 3) = 5$.
E: Simplify the exponents, $(5)^2 = 25$.
The equation now looks like this: $5 + 20 \div 4 \times 25 - 6$.
MD: Perform multiplication and division from left to right, $20 \div 4 = 5$; then $5 \times 25 = 125$.
The equation now looks like this: $5 + 125 - 6$.
AS: Perform addition and subtraction from left to right, $5 + 125 = 130$; then $130 - 6 = 124$

### Example 2

Use the order of operations to evaluate the expression: $14 + 2 \cdot (3 - 1)$.

The first operations to evaluate are any within parenthesis.

$14 + 2 \cdot (3 - 1) = 14 + 2 \cdot 2$

Next, evaluate any multiplication or division.

$14 + 2 \cdot 2 = 14 + 4$

Lastly evaluate any addition or subtraction.

$14 + 4 = 18$

# Computations and Algebraic Relationships

**Additive inverse**

The sum of a number and its **additive inverse**, or opposite, is the additive identity, 0.

<u>Example</u>

Find the additive inverse of

$$3$$
$$-5$$
$$x$$

The additive inverse of 3 is -3 because $3 + (-3) = 0$.
The additive inverse of -5 is 5 because $-5 + 5 = 0$.
The additive inverse of $x$ is $-x$ because $x + (-x) = 0$.

**Multiplicative inverse**

The product of a number and its **multiplicative inverse** is the multiplicative identity, 1. The multiplicative inverse of a number is also called its reciprocal. The reciprocal of a non-zero rational number is also rational. Zero does not have a multiplicative because the product of zero and any number is zero and can therefore not equal 1 and because zero can never be in the denominator of a fraction.

<u>Example</u>

Find the multiplicative inverse of

$$5$$
$$-\frac{2}{3}$$

$x$ such that $x \neq 0$.

The multiplicative inverse of 5 is $\frac{1}{5}$ because $5\left(\frac{1}{5}\right) = 1$.

The multiplicative inverse of $-\frac{2}{3}$ is $-\frac{3}{2}$ because $-\frac{2}{3}\left(-\frac{3}{2}\right) = 1$.

The multiplicative inverse of $x$ is $\frac{1}{x}$ when $x \neq 0$ because $x\left(\frac{1}{x}\right) = 1$ when $x \neq 0$.

<u>Example</u>

An atom of oxygen has eight positively charged protons and eight negatively charged electrons

Determine the charge of an atom of oxygen.

When an atom gains or loses electrons, it becomes an ion. Determine the charge of an oxygen ion which contains two more electrons than an oxygen atom.

An atom of oxygen has a charge of zero because it has the same number of positively charged protons as it does negatively charged electrons: $8 + (-8) = 0$.

An oxygen ion has a charge of -2 because the neutral atom has gained two negatively charged electrons: $0 + (-2) = -2$ or $8 + (-10) = -2$.

Using number lines, show that 2 ½ − 2 ½ = 2 ½ + (−2 ½) = −2 ½ + 2 ½ = 0.

To subtract 2 ½ from 2 ½ on a number line, start at 2 ½ and move two and a half spaces to the left.

$$2 ½ − 2 ½ = 0$$

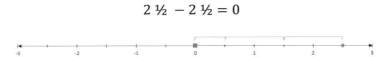

To simplify 2 ½ + (−2 ½) on a number line, start at 2 ½ and move two and a half spaces to the left. 2 ½ + (−2 ½) = 0.

Notice that adding -2 ½ to 2 ½ is that same subtracting 2 ½ from 2 ½.

To add 2 ½ to -2 ½ on a number line, start at -2 ½ and move two and a half spaces to the right.     −2 ½ + 2 ½ = 0

As always, the sum of a number and its opposite is zero.

$$2 ½ − 2 ½ = 2 ½ + (−2 ½) = −2 ½ + 2 ½ = 0$$

## Example

Express each as a positive or negative number. Then, write a phrase to represent the number's opposite.

- A gain of four yards
- A deduction of ten points
- A 5°F drop in temperature
- A debit of $1.60
- An extra half-mile

A gain of four yards → **+4** yards. The opposite is *a loss of four yards*, or **−4** yards.

A deduction of ten points → **−10** points. The opposite is *an addition of 10 points*, or **+10** points.

A 5°F drop in temperature → **−5**°F. The opposite is *an increase in temperature of 5 °F*, or **+5**°F.

A debit of $1.60→ **−$1.60**. The opposite is *a credit of $1.60*, or **+$1.60**.

An extra half-mile→ **+½** mile. The opposite is *a half-mile less*, or **−½** mile

## Ratios to Describe Proportional Situations

As discussed earlier ratios are used to describe how two or more quantities are related. Ratios can also be used to write a proportion or equation, and then solve for some unknown quantity.

<u>Example 1</u>

A recipe for 24 cookies calls for 2 cups of sugar. Find the cups of sugar needed to make 30 cookies.

Using the known quantities, write a ratio relating the cups of sugar to the number of cookies:

$$\frac{2 \; cups}{24 \; cookies}$$

Write a proportion, or equation relating two ratios, and solve for the unknown quantity.

$$\frac{2 \; cups}{24 \; cookies} = \frac{c \; cups}{30 \; cookies}$$

$$60 = 24c$$

$$c = 2\frac{1}{2}$$

Two and a half cups of sugar are needed to make 30 cookies.

<u>Example 2</u>

A map contains a key to relate measurements on the map to real distances. The key on one map says that 2 inches on the map equals 12 miles. Find the distance of a route that is 5 inches long on the map.

Write a proportion that relates the map measurements to real distances. First, write a ratio that relates the information given in the key. The map measurement can be in the numerator, and the real distance in the denominator.

$$\frac{2 \; in}{12 \; mi}$$

Next, write a ratio relating the known map distance to the unknown real distance. The unknown miles can be represented with the letter $m$.

$$\frac{5 \; in}{m \; mi}$$

A proportion is an equation relating two ratios. Write a proportion and solve it for $m$.

$$\frac{2 \; in}{12 \; mi} = \frac{5 \; in}{m \; mi}$$

$$2m = 60$$

$$m = 30$$

The route is 30 miles long.

## Formulating Equations

Being able to formulate an equation is helpful when there are problem situations presented. These will usually be word problems with some known values and an unknown variable that must be solved for.

Example 1

The scale below is balanced. The small blocks each weigh 2 pounds. The large blocks each weigh $p$ pounds.

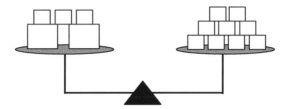

Write an equation showing the relationship between the two sides of the scale.

Given that the two sides of the scale are equal, write an equation relating the blocks on each side of the scale. Represent the weight of each large block with a $p$, and the weight of each small block is 2 pounds.

$2 + 2 + 2 + p + p = 2 + 2 + 2 + 2 + 2 + 2 + 2 + 2 + 2$

Simplify each side of the equation.

$6 + 2p = 18$

Example 2

A band is hired to perform. The band will be paid $4,000. Tickets to watch the band are sold for $10 each. Write an expression showing the difference between the money earned by selling tickets and the cost of hiring the band.

The cost to hire the band is $4,000. The money earned by selling tickets will depend on the number of tickets sold. Let a variable, such as $n$, represent the number of tickets sold. The money earned by selling tickets is the money earned for each ticket, $10, times the number of tickets sold, $n$: $10 \cdot n$. An expression that shows the difference between the money earned by selling tickets and the cost of hiring the band is the money earned minus the band cost: $10 \cdot n - $4,000

## Tables

Tables are presented in a standard format so that they will be easy to read and understand. At the top of the table, there will be a title. This will be a short phrase indicating the information the table or graph intends to convey. The title of a table could be something like "Average Income for Various Education Levels" or "Price of Milk Compared to Demand." A table is composed of information laid out in vertical columns and horizontal rows. Typically, each column will have a label. If "Average Income for Various Education Levels" was placed in a table format, the two columns could be labeled "Education Level" and "Average Income." Each location on the table is called a cell. Cells are defined by their column and row (e.g., second column, fifth row). The table's information is placed in these cells.

<u>Example 1</u>

Use a table to show the relationship between the perimeters of rectangles with the following dimensions:

Rectangle 1: length: $l$, width: $w$
Rectangle 2: length: $l$, width: $2w$
Rectangle 3: length: $l$, width: $3w$
Rectangle 4: length: $l$, width: $4w$

Describe how changing $w$ changed the perimeter of the rectangle.

Create a table showing the dimensions of each rectangle, and the corresponding perimeter.

| Length | Width | Perimeter |
|--------|-------|-----------|
| $l$ | $w$ | $2l + 2w$ |
| $l$ | $2w$ | $2l + 4w$ |
| $l$ | $3w$ | $2l + 6w$ |
| $l$ | $4w$ | $2l + 8w$ |

As $w$ increased by 1, the perimeter increased by $2w$.

<u>Example 2</u>

A kindergarten teacher orders four workbooks for each student. Create a table showing the number of workbooks needed for 1, 2, 3, 4, or 5 students. Then write an equation relating the number of students to the number of workbooks.

The number of workbooks needed increases by four for each additional student. For one student, 4 workbooks are needed.

| Number of students | Number of workbooks |
|--------------------|---------------------|
| 1 | 4 |
| 2 | $4 + 4 = 8$ |
| 3 | $8 + 4 = 12$ |
| 4 | $12 + 4 = 16$ |
| 5 | $16 + 4 = 20$ |

The equation for this table will be in the format of some number of students s equals some number of workbooks w. So for every student there are four more workbooks needed, which means four times the number of students gives us workbooks.

$$4s = w$$

- 24 -

# Geometry and Measurement

**Measurement Conversion**

In math, a conversion refers to changing from one unit of measurement to another. For example to go from inches to feet, the number of inches should be multiplied by twelve since there are twelve inches in a foot.

<u>Example 1</u>

One foot is 12 inches. Convert each of the measurements below:

a) 3 feet in inches

b) 20 inches in feet

Write a ratio to show the relationship between feet and inches. If 1 foot = 12 inches, then a ratio to describe the relationship is: $\frac{1\,ft}{12\,in}$. Use the ratio and write proportions to convert each measure. A variable, such as $x$, can be used to represent the unknown value.

a)

$$\frac{1\,ft}{12\,in} = \frac{3\,ft}{x\,in}$$
$$x = 36$$

3 feet is equal to 36 inches.

b)

$$\frac{1\,ft}{12\,in} = \frac{x\,ft}{20\,in}$$
$$20 = 12x$$
$$x = \frac{20}{12} = \frac{5}{3}$$

20 inches is equal to $\frac{5}{3}$ feet.

<u>Example 2</u>

There are 12 inches in 1 foot, and 3 feet in 1 yard. Convert between the measurements below.

a) 42 inches to feet

b) 15 feet to yards

Write a ratio relating the inches to feet: $\frac{12\,in}{1\,ft}$ and feet to yards: $\frac{3\,ft}{1\,yd}$. Use the ratios to write a proportion to convert the given units.

a) $\frac{12\,in}{1\,ft} = \frac{42\,in}{x\,ft}$. Cross multiply to get $12x = 42$, or $x = 3.5$. Therefore 42 inches = 3.5 feet.

b) $\frac{3\,ft}{1\,yd} = \frac{15\,ft}{x\,yd}$ . Cross multiply to get $3x = 15$, or $x = 5$. Therefore 15 feet = 5 yards.

- 26 -

<u>Example 3</u>

There are 100 cm in 1 m. Convert between the measurements below.

a) 1.4 m in cm

b) 218 cm in m

Write a ratio relating the units: $\frac{100 \text{ cm}}{1 \text{ m}}$. Use the ratio to write a proportion to convert the given units.

a) $\frac{100 \text{ cm}}{1 \text{ m}} = \frac{x \text{ cm}}{1.4 \text{ m}}$. Cross multiply to get $x = 140$. Therefore 1.4 m = 140 cm.

b) $\frac{100 \text{ cm}}{1 \text{ m}} = \frac{218 \text{ cm}}{x \text{ m}}$. Cross multiply to get $100x = 218$, or $x = 2.18$. Therefore 218 cm = 2.18 m.

## Angles in Triangles and Quadrilaterals

The following are relationships involving the angles in triangles and quadrilaterals:

- The sum of the interior angles of a triangle is 180º.
- The smallest angle of a triangle is opposite the shortest side of the triangle. The largest angle of a triangle is opposite the longest side of the triangle.
- The sum of the interior angles of a quadrilateral is 360º.
- Opposite angles of a parallelogram are equivalent.
- A regular quadrilateral is a quadrilateral with four equal sides. The angles of a regular quadrilateral are also equivalent.

## Radius, Diameter, and Circumference

The radius of a circle is half the length of the diameter. The radius of a circle is any line segment drawn from a point on the circle to the circle's center. The diameter of a circle is a line segment draw from one point on a circle to another that goes through the center of the circle. The circumference is the distance around the edge of the circle.

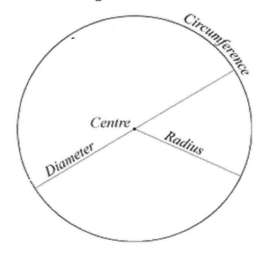

## Graphing Ordered Pairs

An ordered pair is two numbers written in a certain order and usually in parentheses, like (x, y).

Plot the following points on a coordinate plane:

A: (1, 2); B: (5, 3); C: (4, 4)

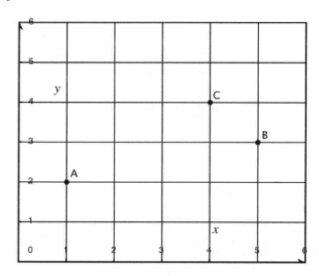

## Area of a parallelogram

The area, $A$, of a parallelogram can be found using the formula $A = bh$, where $b$ is the length of the base and $h$ is the height, which is the distance between the parallelogram's base and its opposite, parallel side. Two congruent triangles are obtained when a parallelogram is cut in half from one of its corners to the opposite corner. From this information, determine the area formula of a triangle.

Two identical triangles make up the parallelogram's area, so the area of one triangle is half the area of the parallelogram. Since the area of a parallelogram is $A = bh$, the area of a triangle is $A = \frac{1}{2}bh$, where $b$ is the base of the triangle and $h$ is the height of the triangle as shown.

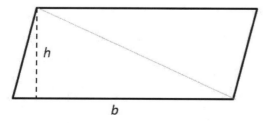
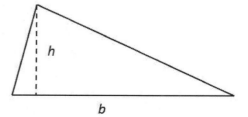

## Area of a trapezoid

The area of a trapezoid is found by the formula $A=12h(b1+b2)$, where A is the area, h is the height (segment joining and perpendicular to the parallel bases), and b1 and b2 are the two parallel sides (bases). Do not use one of the other two sides as the height unless that side is also perpendicular to the parallel bases. The perimeter of a trapezoid is found by the formula $P=a+b1+c+b2$, where P is

- 28 -

the perimeter, and a, b1, c, and b2 are the four sides of the trapezoid. Notice that the height does not appear in this formula.

**Circumference and Diameter**

The formula used to find the circumference, C, of a circle is $C=2\pi r$ or $C=\pi d$, where r is the radius of the circle and d its diameter. To find the diameter of a circle simply draw a line segment from one point on a circle to another that goes through the center of the circle, and measure that distance.

<u>Example</u>

Steve bakes a cake in a pan with a 9-inch diameter. He decides to decorate the cake by placing raspberries around its edge. Each raspberry has a diameter of approximately 0.5 inches. Use the circumference of the cake to estimate how many raspberries Steve needs to purchase.

It may be helpful to begin with a diagram. Looking at the top of the Steve's cake, the view would be:

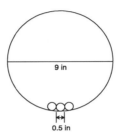

Note that this is not drawn to scale, but is a representation of the problem being solved. To approximate the number of raspberries needed, first find the circumference of the cake. The circumference of a circle is: $2\pi r$, where $r$ is the radius of the circle. To find the radius of the cake, divide the diameter by 2: 9 in ÷ 2 = 4.5 in. The radius of the circle is 4.5 inches. The value pi, $\pi$, can be estimated using the fraction: $\frac{22}{7}$, or 3.14. The circumference of the circle is approximately: $2 \cdot \frac{22}{7} \cdot 4.5 = 28.89$. To find the number of raspberries needed, divide the circumference by the approximate diameter of each raspberry: 28.29 ÷ 0.5 = 56.58. Approximately 57 raspberries will be needed to decorate the cake.

**Perimeter**

The perimeter of a rectangle is the sum of the lengths of its sides.

<u>Example</u>

Draw a rectangle with length: *a* and width: *b*. Describe the perimeter and write an equation to represent the perimeter of the rectangle.

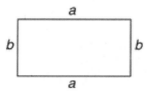

The perimeter of a rectangle is the sum of the length of the sides of the rectangle. The perimeter of the rectangle is: $a + b + a + b$, or $2a + 2b$.

**Area**

The area of a rectangle is the measurement of the inside of the rectangle. The area of a rectangle is found by the formula $A=lw$, where A is the area of the rectangle, l is the length (usually considered to be the longer side) and w is the width (usually considered to be the shorter side). The numbers for l and w are interchangeable.

<u>Example</u>

Draw a rectangle length *x* and width *y*. Describe the area of the rectangle and write an equation to represent the rectangle's area.

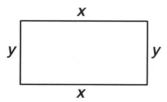

The area of the rectangle is: $x \cdot y$.

<u>Example 2</u>

Leslie decides to tile her bathroom floor with tiles that are rectangles. Each rectangle has a length of 10 inches and a width of 8 inches. Find the number of tiles needed for a floor with an area of 3600 in².

First, find the area of each tile. The area of a rectangle is: $lw$, where *l* is the length of the rectangle, and *w* is the width. The area of each tile is: 10 in · 8 in = 80 in². To find the number of tiles needed, divide the total area of the floor, 3600 in², by the area of each tile: 3600 in² ÷ 80 in² = 45. Leslie needs 45 tiles.

## Volume

The formula for the volume of a prism or a cylinder is $V = Bh$, where $B$ is the area of the base and $h$ is the height of the solid. For a cylinder, the area of the circular base is determined by the formula $B = \pi r^2$. For a prism, the area of the base depends on the shape of the base; for example, a triangular base would have area $\frac{1}{2}bh$, while a rectangular base would have area $bh$.

For a pyramid or cone, the volume is $V = \frac{1}{3}Bh$, where $B$ once again is the area of the base and $h$ is the height. In other words, the volume of a pyramid or cone is one-third the volume of a prism or cylinder with the same base and the same height.

### Example

A bathtub is approximately shaped like a rectangular prism, with no top. The tub has a length of 60 inches, a width of 24 inches, and a height of 16 inches. The tub is filled halfway with water. Find the volume of the water in the tub.

Drawing a diagram may be helpful. Draw a rectangular prism, with $l$ = 60 inches, $w$ = 24 inches, and $h$ = 16 inches. If the tub is filled halfway, then the height of the water is half of the height of the tub, or 16 inches ÷ 2 = 8 inches. Draw a line representing the fill height of the water.

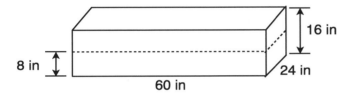

The volume of the water is the volume of the rectangular prism with dimensions: $l$ = 60 in, $w$ = 24 in, and $h$ = 8 in. The volume of a rectangular prism is: $lwh$ = 60 in · 24 in · 8 in = 11,520 in³.

## Area and perimeter of a triangle

The area of a triangle is given by the formula $A = \frac{1}{2}bh$, where $A$ is the area of the triangle, $b$ is the length of the base, and $h$ is the height of the triangle perpendicular to the base. If you know the three sides of a scalene triangle, you can use the formula $A = \sqrt{s(s-a)(s-b)(s-c)}$, where $A$ is the area, $s$ is the semiperimeter $s = \frac{a+b+c}{2}$, and $a$, $b$, and $c$ are the lengths of the three sides. The perimeter of a triangle is given by the formula $P = a + b + c$, where $P$ is the perimeter, and $a$, $b$, and $c$ are the lengths of the three sides. In this case, the triangle may be any shape. The variables $a$, $b$, and $c$ are not exclusive to right triangles in the perimeter formula.

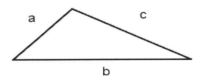

### Equilateral triangles

The area of an equilateral triangle is found by the formula $A = \frac{\sqrt{3}}{4}s^2$, where $A$ is the area and $s$ is the length of a side. You could use the $30° - 60° - 90°$ ratios to find the height of the triangle and then use the standard triangle area formula, but this is faster. The perimeter of an equilateral triangle is found by the formula $P = 3s$, where $P$ is the perimeter and $s$ is the length of a side. If you know the length of the apothem (distance from the center of the triangle perpendicular to the base) and the length of a side, you can use the formula $A = \frac{1}{2}ap$, where $a$ is the length of the apothem and $p$ is the perimeter.

Isosceles triangles

The area of an isosceles triangle is found by the formula, $A = \frac{1}{2}b\sqrt{a^2 - \frac{b^2}{4}}$, where $A$ is the area, $b$ is the base (the unique side), and $a$ is the length of one of the two congruent sides.

If you do not remember this formula, you can use the Pythagorean Theorem to find the height so you can use the standard formula for the area of a triangle.

The perimeter of an isosceles triangle is found by the formula
$A = 2a + b$, where $P$ is the perimeter, $a$ is the length of one of the congruent sides, and $b$ is the base (the unique side).

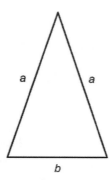

# Data Analysis and Personal Financial Literacy

## Tree Diagram

A tree diagram can be used to find all of the possibilities of a sequence, and are one method for calculating the total number of outcomes in a sample space.

<u>Example</u>

Ted picks his clothing in the morning from a selection of 4 pairs of pants and 3 shirts. Draw a diagram to find the sample space of the selection of an outfit consisting of exactly one pair of pants and one shirt.

> A tree diagram can be used to find the number of different ways pants and shirts can be selected. This will show the sample space for the selection of an outfit.

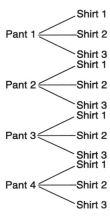

> The sample space is the twelve different combinations of pants and shirts.

## Graphical Representation of Data

Data can be graphed in several different ways depending on how it needs to be presented. These graphs include line plots, line graphs, bar graphs, and stem and leaf plots.

<u>Example 1</u>

A line plot contains quantitative (numerical) values on a number line, with an *x* or dot above each value for the number of times that value is present in a sample.

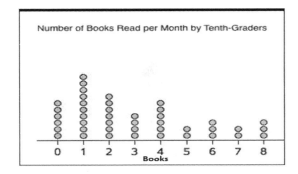

- 33 -

## Example 2

A line graph shows the relationship between two quantities. The data points are connected to show the relationship is continuous. The graph below shows the relationship between time, in hours, and distance traveled by car, in miles. The $x$-axis represents time and the $y$-axis represents total distance traveled.

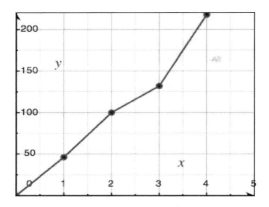

## Example 3

A bar graph is a frequency plot. It contains the frequency of discrete data values, which can either be numerical or categorical (such as a dollar amount or category types, such as types of books).

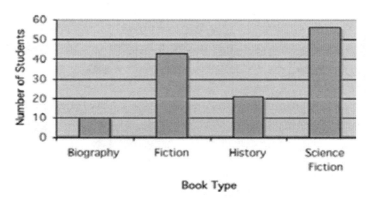

## Example 4

Mr. Glaser records the following grades of students on a 40-point quiz: 18, 27, 29, 30, 34, 35, 35, 37, 40. Represent the data in a stem-and-leaf plot.

The value of the tens place will be the values in the stem, and the value of the ones place will be the values in the leaves. Arrange the values from least to greatest.

| Stem | leaf |
| --- | --- |
| 1 | 8 |
| 2 | 7 9 |

| 3 | 0 4 5 5 7 |
|---|---|
| 4 | 0 |

## Data representation and analysis

Example problem 1

*Represent the following data in a dot plot and find the mode of the data:*

*The amount of money your friends make babysitting per hour*

*5, 2, 7, 9, 4, 5, 6, 7, 9, 7*

*The data is represented in a dot plot below:*

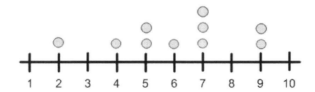

The amount of money your friends make babysitting per hour

This is made by creating a number line that can display the range of data and then placing one dot above each number for each data value equal to that number. The mode of this data is 7, which is the number that occurs in the data most. The mode is easy to see in a dot plot because it is the number that has the most dots. In this data, three people get $7/hour babysitting while only one or two people get paid the other amounts in the list.

Example problem 2

*Represent the following data in a box plot:*

*Michael's math test grades last semester*

*88, 90, 95, 82, 98, 90, 77, 89, 91*

The data is represented in the box plot below:

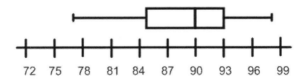

Michael's math test grades last semester

This is made by creating a number line that will fit the distribution of the data and then determining the five points that are needed to create the box plot, which are: the minimum, the maximum, the median, the lower quartile, and the upper quartile. The minimum is the number in the list with the least value, 77, and the maximum is the number with the greatest value, 98. A small tick mark is placed above those two values on the number line. The median of the data is 90, which is found by listing the data in order from least to greatest and finding the number in the middle: $77, 82, 88, 89, 90, 90, 91, 95, 98$. The lower quartile is the median of the lower half of the data, which is 85 because the middle of the lower half of the data is between the two middle numbers 82 and 88, and is therefore found by finding their average: $\frac{82+88}{2} = 85$. The upper quartile is the median of the upper half of the data, which is 93 because it is between 91 and 95, and their average is $\frac{91+95}{2} = 93$. A tick mark is placed above the median and upper and lower quartile values on the number line and a box is created around those three marks. A line is then extended from the ends of the box to the minimum and maximum.

## Interquartile range

The interquartile range of a data set is the difference between the third and first quartiles. That is, one quarter of the data fall below the interquartile range and one quarter of the data above it. Exactly half of the data points fall within the interquartile range, half of those above the median and half below. (This is, of course, why the quartile points are called "quartiles", because they divide the data into quarters: one quarter of the data points are below the first quartile, one quarter between the first and second quartile (the median), and so on.)

The interquartile range is useful to get a rough idea of the spread of the data. The median by itself shows where the data are centered (or rather, shows one measure of central tendency); the interquartile range gives a better idea of how much the data points vary from this center.

## Outlier

An outlier is an extremely high or extremely low value in the data set. It may be the result of measurement error, in which case, the outlier is not a valid member of the data set. However, it may also be a valid member of the distribution. Unless a measurement error is identified, the experimenter cannot know for certain if an outlier is or is not a member of the distribution. There are arbitrary methods that can be employed to designate an extreme value as an outlier. One method designates an outlier (or possible outlier) to be any value less than $Q1-1.5(IQR)$ or any value greater than $Q3+1.5(IQR)$, where Q1 and Q3 are the first and third quartiles and IQR is the interquartile range. For instance, in the data set {42, 71, 22, 500, 33, 38, 62, 44, 58, 37, 61, 25}, the point 500 may be considered an outlier, since 500 is greater than 101.25 (61.5 + 1.5(26.5) = 101.25).

## Mean, Median, Mode, and Range

The mean of a data set is the average of the values. It is found by summing the data points and dividing by the total number of points. The median is the middle-most data value. It is found by first arranging the data from least to greatest. If there are an odd number of data points, the median is the middle-most point. If there is an even number of data points, it is the average of the two middle-most points. The mode of a data set is the data value that is repeated the most. The range of a data set is the difference between the greatest data point and least data point.

## Example 1

Ten students in Mrs. Mason's class record their ages in months: 163, 179, 165, 180, 158, 180, 179, 174, 180, and 165. Find the mean, median, mode, and range of the ages of the students.

The mean is the average age. Sum the ages and divide by 10, the number of ages.

$$\frac{163 + 179 + 165 + 180 + 158 + 180 + 179 + 174 + 180 + 165}{10} = \frac{1723}{10} = 172.3$$

The median is the middle-most data point. First sort the ages from least to greatest:

158, 163, 165, 165, 174, 179, 179, 180, 180, 180.

There is an even number of data points, so the median is the average of the two middle-most data points.

$$\frac{174 + 179}{2} = 176.5$$

The mode is the most frequent age, 180 months.

The range is the difference between the greatest and least data points: 180 – 158 = 22 months.

## Example 2

A company boasts that its mean starting salary is $61,000. Here is the list of the starting salaries on which the company based its claim.

New Employee Starting Salary

| A | $27,000; | B | $29,000 |
|---|---|---|---|
| C | $37,000; | D | $42,000 |
| E | $45,000; | F | $49,000 |
| G | $55,000; | H | $60,000 |
| I | $92,000; | J | $110,000 |
| K | $125,000 | | |

Determine what a smart job seeker should inquire about when presented with a mean starting salary figure.

The company presents $61,000 as the mean starting salary, which is entirely accurate but somewhat misleading since more than 70% of the new employees had starting salaries below $61,000. A smart job seeker will inquire about the median starting salary as this is a better indicator of the salary that can be expected, since this will not inflated by salaries that are much larger or lower than the average.

The median salary in this case is $49,000. This is likely to be closer to the starting salary of an average employee.

# Mathematics Practice Test #1

## Practice Questions

1. Antonio wants to buy a roll of border to finish an art project. At four different shops, he found four different borders he liked. He wants to use the widest of the borders. The list shows the width, in inches, of the borders he found.

$$1\frac{7}{10}, 1.72, 1\frac{3}{4}, 1.695$$

Which roll of border should Antonio buy if he wants to buy the widest border?

  a. $1\frac{7}{10}$
  b. 1.72
  c. $1\frac{3}{4}$
  d. 1.695

2. Daniella wrote a decimal and a fraction which were equivalent to each other. Which pair of numbers could be the pair Daniella wrote?

  a. $0.625, \frac{7}{8}$
  b. $0.375, \frac{3}{8}$
  c. $0.75, \frac{7}{5}$
  d. $0.45, \frac{4}{5}$

3. Which expression best shows the prime factorization of 750?

  a. $2 \times 3 \times 5^3$
  b. $2 \times 3 \times 5^2$
  c. $2 \times 3 \times 5 \times 25$
  d. $2 \times 3 \times 5^2 \times 25$

4. Large boxes of canned beans hold 24 cans of beans and small boxes hold 12 cans. One afternoon, Gerald brought 4 large boxes of canned beans and 6 small boxes of canned beans to the food bank. How many cans of beans did Gerald bring to the food bank that afternoon?

  a. 168
  b. 192
  c. 288
  d. 360

5. Enrique used a formula to find the total cost, in dollars, for repairs he and his helper, Jenny, made to a furnace. The expression below shows the formula he used, with 4 being the number of hours he worked on the furnace and 2 being the number of hours Jenny worked on the furnace.

$$20 + 35(4 + 2) + 47$$

What is the total cost for repairing the furnace?
    a. $189
    b. $269
    c. $277
    d. $377

6. A display at the bottom of the laptop computer Erica was using showed that the battery had a 70% charge. Which decimal is equivalent to 70%?
    a. 0.07
    b. 70.0
    c. 7.0
    d. 0.7

7. The drawing shows a chart used to record completed Math assignments. A checkmark is used to show which assignments are finished.

Math Assignment

Which of the following shows the percentage of Math assignments in the chart which are finished?
    a. 15%
    b. 25%
    c. 55%
    d. 75%

8. Harold learned that 6 out of 10 students at his school live within two miles of the school. If 240 students attend Grade 6 at his school, about how many of these students should Harold expect to live within two miles of the school?
    a. 24
    b. 40
    c. 144
    d. 180

9. A unit of liquid measure in the English System of Measure is the gill. The table, shown here, gives conversions from gills to fluid ounces.

**Conversion Table**

| Gills | Fluid Ounces |
|-------|--------------|
| 2 | 8 |
| 4 | 16 |
| 5 | 20 |
| 6 | 24 |
| 10 | 40 |

Which equation best describes the relationship between gills, $g$, and fluid ounces, $f$?

    a. $f = 8g - 8$
    b. $f = 2g + 4$
    c. $f = 4g$
    d. $4f = g$

10. The table below shows changes in the area of several trapezoids as the lengths of the bases, $b_1$ and $b_2$, remain the same and the height, $h$, changes.

Trapezoids

| $b_1$ (in feet) | $b_2$ (in feet) | $h$ (in feet) | $A$ (in square feet) |
|-----------------|-----------------|---------------|----------------------|
| 5 | 7 | 2 | 12 |
| 5 | 7 | 4 | 24 |
| 5 | 7 | 6 | 36 |
| 5 | 7 | 8 | 48 |

Which formula best represents the relationship between $A$, the areas of these trapezoids, and $h$, their heights?

    a. $A = 5h$
    b. $A = 6h$
    c. $A = 7h$
    d. $A = 12h$

11. A trash company charges a fee of $80 to haul off a load of trash. There is also a charge of $0.05 per mile the load must be hauled. Which equation can be used to find $c$, the cost for hauling a load of trash $m$ miles?

    a. $80(m + 0.05)$
    b. $0.05(m + 80)$
    c. $80m + 0.05$
    d. $0.05m + 80$

12. In ΔRST, shown here, **m∠S** is 20° less than **m∠R**.

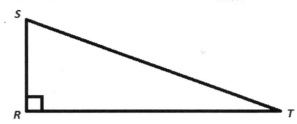

What is the measure of ∠T?
- a. 110°
- b. 70°
- c. 50°
- d. 20°

13. Use this grid to answer the question.

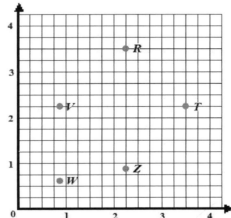

Which ordered pair best represents the coordinates of Point R?
- a. $(2\frac{1}{4}, 3\frac{1}{2})$
- b. $(3\frac{1}{2}, 2\frac{1}{4})$
- c. $(9, 14)$
- d. $(14, 9)$

14. This drawing shows an equilateral triangle and a ruler.

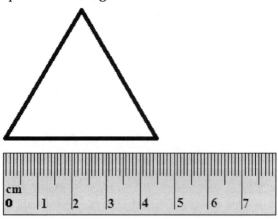

Which is closest to the perimeter of the triangle?
    a. 4.5 centimeters
    b. 9.0 centimeters
    c. 13.5 centimeters
    d. 20.3 centimeters

15. Stephen researched the topic of solar-powered lights for his science project. He exposed 10 new solar lights to five hours of sunlight. He recorded the number of minutes each light continued to shine after dark in the list below.

**63, 67, 73, 75, 80, 91, 63, 72, 79, 87**

Which of these numbers is the mean of the number of minutes in Stephen's list?
    a. 28
    b. 63
    c. 74
    d. 75

16. Grade 6 students at Fairview Middle School were asked to name their favorite of six school subjects. The plot below shows a summary of their answers. Each X represents 5 students.

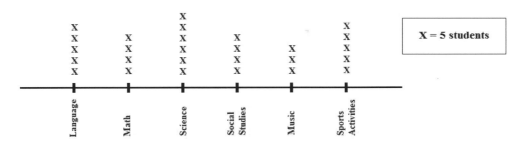

Which graph best represents the data in the plot?

a.

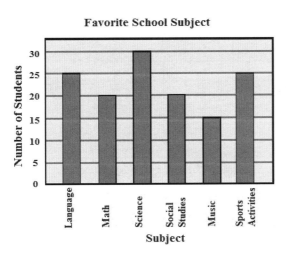

c.

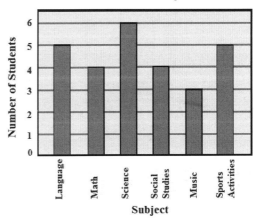

b.

d.

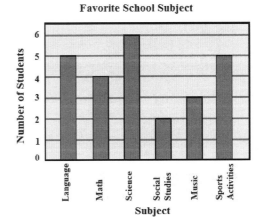

17. Petra installed 10 light fixtures at a new warehouse that was being built. Each of the fixtures required 3 light bulbs. The bulbs come in packages of 5 and cost $8 per package. What was the total cost for the bulbs required for all of the fixtures Petra installed at the warehouse?

    a. $16
    b. $48
    c. $120
    d. $240

18. Anna and other members of her club sold caps to commemorate their city's 100th birthday. The caps sold for $14 and came in four colors. The club made $3,360 in total sales from selling the caps. The graph below shows the part of the total sales that each color represented.

**Colors of Caps Sold**

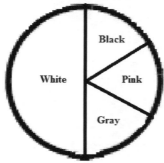

Which number is closest to the combined number of white and pink caps sold by Anna's club members?

    a. 40
    b. 80
    c. 120
    d. 160

19. Jason wants to put dry fertilizer on the grass in his front yard. The yard is 20 feet wide and 45 feet long. Each pound of the fertilizer he plans to use is enough for 150 square feet. Which procedure could Jason use to determine the correct amount of fertilizer to use on the entire yard?

    a. Divide 150 by 20 and divide 150 by 45, and then add those quotients together
    b. Add 20 and 45, double that total, and then divide that total by 150
    c. Multiply 20 by 45, and then subtract 150 from that product
    d. Multiply 20 by 45, and then divide that product by 150

20. Tomas needs $100 to buy a telescope he wants. He received $40 as a gift and spent $10 on a book about telescopes. He earned $35 doing small jobs for his family. The steps Tomas can use to find the amount he still needs to save to buy the telescope are shown here in incorrect order.

Step R: Subtract 65 from 100.
Step S: Subtract 10 from 40.
Step T: Add 35 to 30.

Which sequence shows the steps in the correct order?

    a. T, S, R
    b. T, R, S
    c. S, T, R
    d. R, S, T

21. Place your answer on the provided griddable answer sheet.

Kerianne collected the weights of her friends. What is the range of her friends' weight?

55 lbs, 63 lbs, 48 lbs, 72 lbs, 61 lbs, 68 lbs

22. Candace's shoelace broke. She measured the unbroken shoelace and finds that she needs a replacement lace that is at least 16 inches long. The store has the following lengths available.

$$15\frac{7}{10}, 16.25, \frac{47}{3}, 15.5$$

Which one of the following lace lengths would be long enough to replace the broken shoelace?

    a. $15\frac{7}{10}$
    b. 16.25
    c. $\frac{47}{3}$
    d. 15.5

23. Nadia is working summer jobs. She earns $5 for every dog she walks, $2 for bringing back a trashcan, $1 for checking the mail, and $5 for watering the flowers. Nadia walks 3 dogs, brings back 5 trashcans, checks the mail for 10 neighbors, and waters the flowers at 6 houses. Which expression can be used to find out how much money Nadia earned?

    a. $2(5) +$6(10) + $1
    b. $10(6) + $1 + $5
    c. $5(3+6) + $2(5) + $1(10)
    d. $15 + $10 + $16

24. Only 8% of the dogs were solid white. Which decimal is equivalent to 8%?

    a. 0.08
    b. 80.0
    c. 8.0
    d. 0.8

25. Use this grid to answer the question.

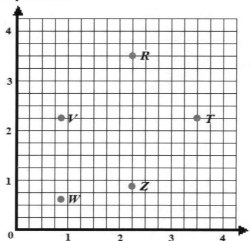

Which of the points on the grid best represents the point at $(2\frac{1}{4}, \frac{7}{8})$?

    a. T
    b. V
    c. W
    d. Z

26. Place your answer on the provided griddable answer sheet.

The recipe called for 2 pints of milk. How many cups of milk are needed?

27. Using the number line below, which of the following comparisons is correct?

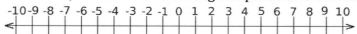

    a. -7 > -4
    b. 8 > 10
    c. -3 > -6
    d. -2 < -10

28. Which of the following lists of rational numbers is listed in increasing order?

    a. $0, 2, 4, \frac{7}{2}, 6$
    b. $0, \frac{1}{2}, \frac{1}{3}, \frac{1}{4}, 1$
    c. $-3, \frac{-9}{2}, -1, 4, 10$
    d. $-2, \frac{-3}{2}, -1, \frac{5}{4}, 2$

29. The Morgan family consists of six members. The family wants to share a ten-pound bag of candy equally. Which of the following does NOT correctly represent the division problem that is necessary to determine how much each family member should receive?

    a. $10 \div 6$

    b. $\frac{6}{10}$

    c. $10 \times \frac{1}{6}$

    d. $\frac{10}{6}$

30. Which of the following is equivalent to $\frac{4}{3}$?

    a. $4 \div 3$

    b. $4 \times \frac{1}{3}$

    c. Both of these options are equivalent.

    d. Neither of these options is equivalent.

31. Which of the following expressions is equivalent to $4 + 6 \cdot 3 + 2$?

    a. $8 \cdot 3 + 2 \cdot 1$

    b. $4^2 + 2 \cdot 4$

    c. $2 \cdot 3^2 + 3 \cdot 4$

    d. $2 + (6 - 4) \cdot 10$

32. Which of the following is a numeric expression?

    a. $2 + 5$

    b. $7 + x$

    c. Ethan is 2 years older than Kyle.

    d. $x + 1 = 4$

33. Which of the following expressions is equivalent to $2(a + 3) + 3a + 4$?

    a. $5a + 10$

    b. $5a + 7$

    c. $4a + 10$

    d. $12a$

34. Rafael purchased 8 new tires for the two family cars. The price of each tire was $144, including taxes. He agreed to make 18 equal monthly payments, interest-free, to pay for the tires. What will be the amount Rafael should pay each month?

    a. $16

    b. $32

    c. $64

    d. $128

35. A farmer had about 150 bags of potatoes on his trailer. Each bag contained from 23 to 27 pounds of potatoes. Which is the best estimate of the total number of pounds of potatoes on the farmer's trailer?

    a. 3,000

    b. 3,700

    c. 4,100

    d. 5,000

36. Which of the following algebraic representations is a multiplicative relationship?

    a. $y = 3x$
    b. $y = x + 3$
    c. $y = x$
    d. $y = x + 1$

37. Which of the following numeric representations is an additive relationship?

a.

| X | y |
|---|---|
| 0 | 0 |
| 2 | 4 |
| 4 | 8 |
| 6 | 12 |

c.

| x | y |
|---|---|
| 1 | 5 |
| 2 | 10 |
| 3 | 15 |
| 4 | 20 |

b.

| x | y |
|---|---|
| 1 | 3 |
| 2 | 4 |
| 3 | 5 |
| 4 | 6 |

d.

| x | y |
|---|---|
| 1 | 3 |
| 3 | 9 |
| 5 | 15 |
| 7 | 21 |

38. Which of the following equations represents the relationship shown in this table?

| x | y |
|---|---|
| 1 | 7 |
| 2 | 8 |
| 3 | 9 |
| 5 | 11 |

    a. $y = 6x$
    b. $y = 5x + 6$
    c. $y = x + 5$
    d. $y = x + 6$

39. Which of the following statements in NOT true about the relationship represented by the graph below?

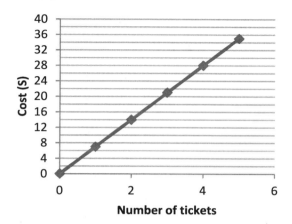

a. The number of tickets is graphed on the x-axis.
b. The cost is the independent variable.
c. The cost of two tickets is $14.
d. The cost increases as the number of tickets increases.

40. Which of the following representations is equivalent to $y = x + 4$?

a.

| x | 3 | 5 | 10 | 15 |
|---|---|---|----|----|
| y | 7 | 9 | 14 | 19 |

b.

| x | 1 | 2 | 3 | 4 |
|---|---|---|----|----|
| y | 4 | 8 | 12 | 16 |

c.

| x | 10 | 11 | 12 | 14 |
|---|----|----|----|----|
| y | 6 | 7 | 8 | 9 |

d.

| x | 0 | 6 | 12 | 18 |
|---|---|----|----|----|
| y | 0 | 12 | 24 | 36 |

- 49 -

41. Which of the following equations or inequalities represents this scenario?

The cost of a gallon of gasoline has been over $2.75 during the month of July.

    a. $x = 2.75$
    b. $x > 2.75x$
    c. $x > 2.75$
    d. $x < 2.75$

42. Which of the following is the correct representation for the solution of $x + 2 = 5$?

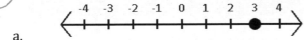

    a.

    b.

    c.

    d.

43. Which of the following is the correct representation for the solution of $x + 3 < 4$?

    a.

    b.

    c.

    d.

44. Which one of the following equations or inequalities and its corresponding solution models the following problem?

Jessica spends $31.00 on four t-shirts that were on sale for the exact same price. Write and solve an equation or inequality to determine the cost of each t-shirt.

    a. $4x < 31.00$; $x < 7.75$
    b. $4x = 31.00$; $x = 7.75$
    c. $4 + x = 31.00$; $x = 27.00$
    d. $4x > 31.00$; $x > 7.75$

45. Which of the following mathematical statements and corresponding solutions best models the following problem?

Josiah needs at least $240 for a new cell phone. He has already earned $160. Write and solve an inequality to represent the amount of money Josiah still needs to earn.

   a. $160 + x = 240; x = 80$
   b. $160 \geq 240 + x; x < 80$
   c. $x \geq 240 + 160; x \geq 400$
   d. $x \geq 240 - 160; x \geq 80$

46. The rectangular floor of a garage has an area of 198 square feet. Andy knows that the floor is 7 feet longer than it is wide. What is length of the floor of the garage?

   a. 11 feet
   b. 14 feet
   c. 18 feet
   d. 92 feet

47. What is the interquartile range, or IQR, of the data summarized in the box-and-whisker plot below?

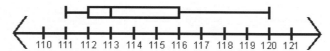

   a. 9
   b. 4
   c. 113
   d. 3

48. Tyler gathers information about checking accounts offered by four different financial institutions. Which institution offers a student checking account with no monthly service fee and a free debit card?

| Financial Institution #1 | Financial Institution #2 | Financial Institution #3 | Financial Institution #4 |
|---|---|---|---|
| Basic Checking with a $10 a month fee if the account falls below $100 Student checking with $1 monthly service fee Debit cards: free for all accounts Fee of $3 for using ATMs from other institutions Overdraft fee of $25 | Basic checking with a $5 monthly service fee Student checking with $2 monthly service fee Debit cards: $0.15 service charge for each purchase Fee of $1 for using ATMs from other institutions Overdraft fee of $30 | Basic checking with a $10 monthly service fee Student checking with $5 monthly service fee Debit cards: $0.25 service charge for each purchase Fee of $2 for using ATMs from other institutions Overdraft fee of $50 | Basic Checking with a $20 a month fee if the account falls below $100 Student checking with no monthly service fee Debit cards: free to all accounts Fee of $1 for using ATMs from other institutions Overdraft fee of $20 |

   a. Financial Institution #1
   b. Financial Institution #2
   c. Financial Institution #3
   d. Financial Institution #4

49. Which of the following characteristics is NOT true concerning a debit card?

    a. Debit cards are convenient to use.
    b. Fees are often applied if the account is overdrawn.
    c. The buyer purchases and pays for the item immediately.
    d. Money for the purchase is a loan that must be repaid later.

50. Which of the following characteristics is true for both debit and credit cards?

    a. Interest fees are applied if the account is not paid off every month.
    b. Items are purchased now and paid for later.
    c. They are convenient to use.
    d. Money is withdrawn directly from the cardholder's account at the time of purchase.

51. What is the balance of this check register after the transaction on 6/22?

| Number or code | Date | Description of transaction | Withdrawal/ Payment/Fee (-) | | Deposit/ Credit (+) | | Balance | |
|---|---|---|---|---|---|---|---|---|
| | 6/1 | | | | | | 150 | 00 |
| | 6/3 | Online payment to School Lunch Program | 25 | 00 | | | | |
| | 6/7 | ATM withdrawal from my bank | 20 | 00 | | | | |
| | 6/13 | Deposited babysitting job | | | 24 | 00 | | |
| 117 | 6/15 | Donation to Dog Shelter | 10 | 00 | | | | |
| | 6/20 | Deposit from cleaning job | | | 40 | 00 | | |
| | 6/22 | Transfer to savings | 60 | 00 | | | | |
| | | | | | | | | |

    a. $104
    b. $99
    c. $329
    d. $101

52. Which of the following information is included in a credit report?

    a. Personal information, including name, address and employer
    b. Bank loans that are past due
    c. Account information, such as mortgages and car loans
    d. All of the above

# Answers and Explanations

## TEKS Standard (6.2)(D)

**1. C:** To answer this question correctly, convert all numbers to decimal form to make them easy to compare. Since two of the numbers are already in decimal form, we only need to convert $1\frac{7}{10}$ and $1\frac{3}{4}$ to decimal form.

$$7 \div 10 = 0.7, \text{ so } 1\frac{7}{10} = 1.7$$
$$\text{and } 3 \div 4 = 0.75, \text{ so } 1\frac{3}{4} = 1.75$$

Therefore, by comparing place values from left to right of 1.7, 1.72, 1.75 and 1.695, we see that 1.695 is least, 1.7 is next greatest, 1.72 is next, and 1.75 is greatest. So, Antonio should buy the border that is $1\frac{3}{4}$ inches wide.

## TEKS Standard (6.4)(G)

**2. B:** To answer this question, one method that can be used is to convert all the fractions to decimal form so it is easier to compare them to each other. This can be done by simply dividing, since the fraction sign means division.

$$7 \div 8 = 0.875$$
$$3 \div 8 = 0.375$$
$$7 \div 5 = 1.4$$
$$4 \div 5 = 0.8$$

So, the only pair of numbers in which the fraction is equivalent to the decimal is in answer B.

## TEKS Standard (6.7)(A)

**3. A:** There is more than one way to solve this problem. One method is to use the fact that the number ends in 0. This means 10 is a factor. So, 10 × 75 = 750. The factor 10 has prime factors of 2 and 5. The factor 75 has factors of 3 and 25 and the 25 has two factors of 5. Putting the prime factors in order, least to greatest, and showing the three factors of 5 with an exponent of 3 gives us answer A: $2 \times 3 \times 5^3$.

## TEKS Standard (6.3)(D)

**4. A:** Multiply 24 by 4 to get 96 and multiply 12 by 6 to get 72. Then, add 96 and 72 to get the correct answer, 168.

## TEKS Standard (6.3)(D)

**5. C:** To solve this formula, follow the order of operations. First, add what is in the parenthesis, 4 + 2, to get 6. Then, multiply the 6 by 35 to get 210. Last, we should add 20 + 210 + 47 to get 277.

## TEKS Standard (6.4)(G)

**6. D:** To correctly write a percent as a decimal, the percent sign is dropped and the number is rewritten with the decimal point two places to the left. This is because a percent is always a value out of 100 and the second place after the decimal point is the hundredths place. So, 70% = 0.70 and the zero at the end after the decimal can be dropped.

## TEKS Standard (6.5)(B)

**7. D:** There are 15 of the 20 assignments with check marks indicating a finished assignment. Since the fraction $\frac{1}{20}$ represents 5%, then 15 times 5% gives 75% of the assignments finished.

## TEKS Standard (6.4)(C)

**8. C:** One way to find this answer is to set up a proportion: $\frac{6}{10} = \frac{G}{240}$, in which $G$ represents the number of Grade 6 students living within two miles of the school. To solve the proportion, we should cross-multiply. So, 10 times $G$ = 6 times 240. This gives the equation:

$10G$ = 1,440. To solve the equation we divide both sides of the equation by 10, which gives $G$ = 144.

## TEKS Standard (6.5)(A)

**9. C:** Looking at the chart, a pattern can be seen in the relationship between the number of gills and the number of fluid ounces. Each number of gills in the first column, when multiplied by 4, gives the number of fluid ounces in the second column. So, $f$ equals 4 times $g$, or $f = 4g$.

## TEKS Standard (6.8)(C)

**10. B:** The formula for the area of trapezoids is not necessarily needed here to do this problem. Since the relationship between the area, $A$, and the height, $h$, can be seen in the chart, looking at the third and fourth columns to see if there is a pattern will show a relationship between the variables. Each value in the area column is equal to 6 times the value in the height column. So, we get $A = 6h$.

## TEKS Standard (6.6)(C)

**11. D:** The amount charged for miles hauled will require us to multiply the number of miles by $0.05. The charge for each load of $80 is not changed by the number of miles hauled. That will be added to the amount charged for miles hauled. So, the equation needs to show 0.05 times miles plus 80, or $c = 0.05m + 80$.

## TEKS Standard (6.8)(A)

**12. D:** The box symbol shown at $\angle R$ means that $\angle R$ measures 90°. Since we are told $m\angle S$ is 20° less than $m\angle R$, subtract 90 −20 to get 70. This means that $m\angle S$ = 70°. The sum of $m\angle R$ and $m\angle S$ is found by adding: 90 +70 = 160. The sum of all angles in a triangle always adds up to 180°, so subtracting 180 − 160 results in a difference of 20. So, $m\angle T$ is 20°.

## TEKS Standard (6.11)(A)

**13. A:** Each of the units represents $\frac{1}{4}$ since there are 4 spaces between each unit. The point $R$ is 9 units right of the $y$-axis, or $\frac{9}{4}$, which is equivalent to $2\frac{1}{4}$, and 14 units up from the $x$-axis, or $\frac{14}{4}$, which is equivalent to $3\frac{1}{2}$. An ordered pair always has the $x$-coordinate (how much to the right or left the point is) first, and then the $y$-coordinate (how much up or down the point is). This is why Answer B is incorrect. So, the correct answer is $\left(2\frac{1}{4}, 3\frac{1}{2}\right)$.

## TEKS Standard (6.8)(A)

**14. C:** The ruler is used to determine the length of one side of the triangle, which is about 4.5 centimeters. Since this is an equilateral triangle, all three sides are of equal length. To find the perimeter, we add up all of the sides. However, since they are all the same length, we can just multiply 4.5 centimeters by 3 to get 13.5 centimeters.

## TEKS Standard (6.12)(C)

**15. D:** The mean is just the average. To calculate this, find the total of all 10 numbers by adding. Then, divide that total by 10 because that is the number of data points. The total is 750, so the mean of this group of numbers is 75

## TEKS Standard (6.12)(A)

**16. B:** Notice that the vertical scale should be 0 to 30 by 5's since each of the X's in the plot represent 5 students. Also, each column should represent a number from the line plot. For example, since Language and Sports Activities both show 5 X's, and each X represents 5 students, 5 times 5 = 25. The subjects of Math and Social Studies both show 4 X's, so 4 times 5 = 20. All of the values are found in this way and the only chart that shows these values is B.

## TEKS Standard (6.3)(D)

**17. B:** To answer this question, find the total number of bulbs required by multiplying 10 by 3. The number of packages of bulbs required can be found by dividing this total number of bulbs, 30, by 5, to find that 6 packages are needed. Then, multiplying 6 by the cost per package, 8, we find that the total cost for all the bulbs needed was $48.

## TEKS Standard (6.13)(A)

**18. D:** To answer this question, the total number of caps sold must be found by dividing the total sales, 3,360, by the price of each cap, 14. 3,360 ÷ 14 = 240, so 240 caps were sold in total. So, looking at the graph, it appears that about half of the caps were white, around 120. The graph also shows that the other 3 colors were sold in about equal numbers, so dividing the other half, 120, by 3, gives around 40. Then, adding 120 white caps and 40 pink caps, gives an answer of 160. The club had close to 160 combined sales of white and pink caps.

## TEKS Standard (6.8)(D)

**19. D:** This procedure first finds the area to be fertilized, by multiplying the length and width of the rectangular yard. Then, it divides that area by the area each pound of fertilizer will cover.

## TEKS Standard (6.3)(D)

**20. C:** The first step would be to subtract the $10 he spent on the book from the gift, $40. This gives us $30. This is how much Tomas still has. We add the $35 he earned to the $30 remaining from the gift, which gives $65, the amount Tomas has in total. Then we subtract $65 from the $100 cost of the telescope to find the amount Tomas still needs to save.

## TEKS Standard (6.12)(C)

- 55 -

**21. 24:** Begin by arranging the different weights from least to greatest:

48 lbs, 55 lbs, 61 lbs, 63 lbs 68 lbs, 72 lbs. Range is the difference between the highest and lowest values in a set of data; therefore, 72 − 48 = 24.

### TEKS Standard (6.4)(G)

**22. B:** It is easier to think as the required 16 inches as 16.00 and convert all answer choices to a decimal to compare. Anything greater than 16.00 would be sufficient. $15\frac{7}{10}$ is equal to 15.7, $\frac{47}{3}$ is equivalent to 15.67 and 15.5 remains 15.5. These three choices are all slightly less than the required 16.00 inches; therefore making 16.25 inches the only adequate choice.

### TEKS Standard (6.9)(C)

**23. C:** Since she earns $5 for walking dogs and watering flowers, this term can be combined to simplify the equation. The other terms for bringing back trashcans and checking the mail are straight multiplication.

### TEKS Standard (6.5)(C)

**24. A:** To correctly write a percent as a decimal, the percent sign is dropped and the number is rewritten with the decimal point two places to the left. If there is not two digits in the percent, a zero is used as a place holder. This is because a percent is always a value out of 100 and the second place after the decimal point is the hundredths place. So, 8% = 0.08.

### TEKS Standard (6.11)(A)

**25. D:** Each of the units represents $\frac{1}{4}$. The point Z is 9 units right of the y-axis or $\frac{9}{4}$ units, which is equivalent to $2\frac{1}{4}$. The point R is also 9 units from the y-axis, or $\frac{9}{4}$, which is equivalent to $2\frac{1}{4}$. Be careful to notice that coordinate pairs always come in the order of the x-coordinate and then the y-coordinate, and is defined by the pair of numbers. The y- coordinate for Z is $\frac{7}{8}$, while Point R has a y-coordinate of $3\frac{1}{2}$.

### TEKS Standard (6.4)(H)

**26. 4:** Each pint is equivalent to 2 cups; therefore 2 pints is equivalent to 4 cups.
### TEKS Standard (6.2)(C)

**27. C:** Larger numbers are to the right on a horizontal number line, and smaller numbers are to the left on a horizontal number line. That means -7 < -4, 8 < 10, -3 > -6, and -2 > -10. Therefore, choice C is correct.

### TEKS Standard (6.2)(E)

**28. D:** In choice D $\frac{-3}{2}$ can be rewritten as -1.5, and $\frac{5}{4}$ can be rewritten as 1.25. Thus, choice D can be rewritten as -2, -1.5, -1, 1.25, 2. This list is in increasing order. Therefore, choice D is correct.

### TEKS Standard (6.2)(E)

- 56 -

**29. B:** To determine the amount of candy each family member receives, divide 10 by 6. Division can be represented in various ways. A division problem such as $a \div b$ can be written as the fraction $\frac{a}{b}$ if $b \neq 0$. So, 10 divided by 6 is written as $\frac{10}{6}$. Therefore, choice B is correct.

### TEKS Standard (6.2)(E)

**30. C:** Division can be represented in various ways. A division problem such as $a \div b$ can be written as the fraction $\frac{a}{b}$ if $b \neq 0$. Specifically, $4 \div 3$ can be represented as $\frac{4}{3}$, and $\frac{4}{3}$ can be written as $4 \times \frac{1}{3}$. Therefore, choice C is correct.

### TEKS Standard (6.7)(D)

**31. B:** The correct order of operations is found by the expression _Please Excuse My Dear Aunt Sally (PEMDAS)_, which represents parentheses, exponents, multiplication or division, and addition or subtraction. In the expression $4 + 6 \cdot 3 + 2$, the multiplication is completed first, yielding $4 + 18 + 2$ or 24. In choice B, the exponent is applied first, yielding $16 + 2 \cdot 4$. The multiplication is performed next, yielding $16 + 8$ or 24. Therefore, choice B is correct.

### TEKS Standard (6.7)(B)

**32. A:** Numeric expressions contain only numbers and operators. The option "2 + 5" is a numeric expression. The option "$7 + x$" is an algebraic expression. The statement "Ethan is 2 years older than Kyle" is a verbal expressions. The statement "$x + 1 = 4$" is an algebraic equation. Therefore, choice A is correct.

### TEKS Standard (6.7)(D)

**33. A:** Applying the distributive property to $2(a + 3) + 3a + 4$ yields $2a + 6 + 3a + 4$. Combining like terms yields $5a + 10$. Therefore, choice A is correct.

### TEKS Standard (6.3)(D)

**34. C:** First, multiply the cost of each tire, $144, by the number of tires, 8, to get $1,152. Then, divide $1,152 by the number of months, 18, to get the amount paid each month, $64.

### TEKS Standard (6.3)(D)

**35. B:** 3,700 is the only answer between the minimum number of potatoes that could have been on the trailer, 150 X 23= 3,450, and the maximum number of potatoes that could have been on the trailer, 27 X 150 = 4,050. Another method that could be used to answer this question is to multiply 25, the number halfway between 23 and 27, by 150. The product, 3,750 is very near the correct answer.

### TEKS Standard (6.4)(C)

**36. A:** Additive relationships have the form $y = x + a$. Multiplicative relationships have the form $y = ax$. The algebraic representation $y = 3x$ is in the form $y = ax$, where $a = 3$. Therefore, choice A is correct.

### TEKS Standard (6.4)(F)

**37. B:** In Table $A$, $y$ results from $x$ being multiplied by 2. In the Table $B$, $y$ results from 2 being added to $x$. In Table $C$, $y$ results from $x$ being multiplied by 5. In Table $D$, $y$ results from $x$ being multiplied by 3. Tables $A$, $C$, and $D$ represent multiplicative relationships. Table $B$ represents an additive relationship. Therefore, choice B is correct.

### TEKS Standard (6.6)(A)

**38. D:** The $x$ is the independent variable. The $y$ is the dependent variable. From the table, we can see that $y$ increases as $x$ increases. The $y$-values are obtained by adding 6 to the $x$-values. Therefore, choice D is correct.

### TEKS Standard (6.6)(C)

**39. B:** The number of tickets, which is graphed on the $x$-axis, is the independent variable. The cost, which is graphed on the $y$-axis, is the dependent variable. The cost of two tickets is $14. Therefore, choice B is correct.

### TEKS Standard (6.6)(C)

**40. A:** In table $A$, $y$ results from 4 being added to $x$. In table $B$, $y$ results from $x$ being multiplied by 4. In table $C$, $y$ results from 4 being subtracted from $x$. In table $D$, $y$ results from $x$ being multiplied by 2. Therefore, choice A is correct.

### TEKS Standard (6.9)(A)

**41. C:** Let $x$ represent the cost of one gallon of gasoline. Since the cost of gasoline has been over $2.75 during the month of July, the cost of gasoline has been greater than $2.75. This can be represented as $x > 2.75$.

### TEKS Standard (6.9)(B)

**42. A:** The equation $x + 2 = 5$ can be solved by subtracting 2 from both sides of the equation. This results in $x = 3$. This is represented by a solid circle at 3 on a number line. Therefore, choice A is correct.

### TEKS Standard (6.9)(B)

**43. A:** The inequality $x + 3 < 4$ can be solved by subtracting 3 from both sides of the inequality. This results in $x < 1$. This solution is represented on a number line by an open circle at 1 and an arrow pointing to the left. Therefore, choice A is correct.

### TEKS Standard (6.10)(A)

**44. B:** If we let $x$ represent the cost of each t-shirt, then $4x = 31.00$. This equation can be solved by dividing both sides by four, which results in $x = 7.75$. Therefore, choice B is correct.

### TEKS Standard (6.10)(B)

**45. D:** Josiah has earned $160. He needs at least $240 – $160 more. This can be represented by the inequality $x \geq 240 - 160$, which can be simplified to $x \geq 80$. If Josiah earns $80 or more, he will have enough money to purchase the cell phone. Therefore, choice D is correct.

### TEKS Standard (6.8)(D)

**46. C:** Guess and check is one way to find the correct answer. We know the length times the width gives the area of the garage floor, 198 square feet. We might guess that the width is 9. We know that the length is 7 more than the width, so, then the length would be 16. 9 times 16 is 144. We would see that our first guess is too low, so we guess higher. We might guess 12 for the width. The length is 7 more, so the length would be 19. 12 times 19 is 228, but this is too high. When we try 11 for the width, we find the length to be 18. 11 times 18 is 198, so the width of the garage floor is 11 and the length is 18. Be careful to note that the question asks for the length and not the width.

### TEKS Standard (6.13)(A)

**47. B:** The IQR is the difference between $Q_1$ and $Q_3$. Quartile 1, marked by the lower boundary of the box, is 112. Quartile 3, marked by the upper boundary of the box, is 116. The IQR = 116 – 112, or 4. Therefore, choice B is correct.

### TEKS Standard (6.14)(A)

**48. D:** Both Financial Institution #1 and #4 offer free debit cards, but only Financial Institution #4 also has student checking with no service fee. Therefore, choice D is correct.

### TEKS Standard (6.14)(B)

**49. D:** When using a debit card, the money is withdrawn directly from the cardholder's account. When using a credit card, money for the purchase is a loan that must be repaid later. Therefore, choice D is correct.

### TEKS Standard (6.14)(B)

**50. C:** Credit cards have interest fees that are applied if the account is not paid off every month. With credit cards, items are purchased now and paid for later. Both debit and credit cards are convenient to use. With debit cards, money is withdrawn directly from the cardholder's account at the time of purchase. Therefore, choice C is correct.

### TEKS Standard (6.14)(C)

**51. B:** Deposits are added to the balance. Withdrawals are subtracted from the balance. The check register is completed below. The balance after the transaction on 6/22 is $99, so choice B is correct.

| Number or code | Date | Description of transaction | Withdrawal/ Payment/Fee (-) | | Deposit/ Credit (+) | | Balance | |
|---|---|---|---|---|---|---|---|---|
| | 6/1 | | | | | | 150 | 00 |
| | 6/3 | Online payment to School Lunch Program | 25 | 00 | | | 125 | 00 |
| | 6/7 | ATM withdrawal from my bank | 20 | 00 | | | 105 | 00 |
| | 6/13 | Deposited babysitting job | | | 24 | 00 | 129 | 00 |
| 117 | 6/15 | Donation to Dog Shelter | 10 | 00 | | | 119 | 00 |
| | 6/20 | Deposit from cleaning job | | | 40 | 00 | 159 | 00 |
| | 6/22 | Transfer to savings | 60 | 00 | | | 99 | 00 |
| | | | | | | | | |

### TEKS Standard (6.14)(F)

**52. D:** Credit reports contain detailed information, including personal information (name, address, and employer); public records, including civil judgements; negative items, such as accounts sent to collections; bank loans that are past due; accounts in good standing, such as mortgage and car loans; and any previous credit history inquiries. Therefore, choice D is correct.

# Mathematics Practice Test #2

## Practice Questions

1. Four students measured the length of the pencil each was using. The list shows the lengths, in centimeters, of the four pencils.

17.03 cm, 17.4 cm, 17.31 cm, 17.09 cm

Which list shows the lengths of the pencils in order, from shortest to longest?

    a. 17.4 cm, 17.31 cm, 17.09 cm, 17.03 cm
    b. 17.03 cm, 17.09 cm, 17.4 cm, 17.31 cm
    c. 17.4 cm, 17.03 cm, 17.09 cm, 17.31 cm
    d. 17.03 cm, 17.09 cm, 17.31 cm, 17.4 cm

2. Castor collects only baseball and football cards. He has 40 baseball cards and 10 football cards. Which decimal best shows the part of his entire card collection represented by his baseball cards?

    a. 0.8
    b. 0.75
    c. 0.4
    d. 0.25

3. Which expression best shows the prime factorization of 630?

    a. $2 \times 3 \times 105$
    b. $2 \times 5 \times 7 \times 9$
    c. $2 \times 3^2 \times 5 \times 7$
    d. $2^2 \times 3^2 \times 5 \times 7$

4. A club is making necklaces in school colors. They plan to use an equal number of blue beads and silver beads on each necklace. The blue beads come in bags of 60 and the silver beads come in bags of 80. What is the smallest number of bags of each color the club can purchase to have an equal number of each color bead with no beads left when the necklaces are finished?

    a. 3 bags of blue and 4 bags of silver
    b. 4 bags of blue and 3 bags of silver
    c. 40 bags of blue and 30 bags of silver
    d. 80 bags of blue and 60 bags of silver

5. One cold afternoon at a small café, 20 people drank hot tea, 45 drank coffee, and 15 drank hot chocolate. Which ratio compares the number of people who drank coffee to the number who drank tea?

    a. 4 to 13
    b. 4 to 9
    c. 9 to 4
    d. 3 to 1

6. A lake near Armando's home is reported to be 80% full of water. Which fraction is equivalent to 80% and in simplest form?

   a. $\frac{1}{80}$

   b. $\frac{8}{10}$

   c. $\frac{4}{5}$

   d. $\frac{80}{1}$

7. The rectangle in this drawing is divided into equal-sized parts, with some of them shaded a darker color.

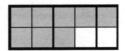

What percent best represents the part of the rectangle that is shaded a darker color?

   a. 8%
   b. 20%
   c. 53%
   d. 80%

8. Annette read that out of 20 televisions sold in her state last year, 3 were Brand V. If a furniture store near her home sold 360 televisions last year, about how many should Annette expect to be Brand V?

   a. 18
   b. 54
   c. 1,080
   d. 2,400

9. Julia has a cell phone contract with a monthly charge of $45. She bought a phone with a one-time price of $50 with that contract. Which table best represents the total of all charges which should be paid at the end of each month of the contract?

a.

| Number of Months | 1 | 2 | 3 | 4 | 5 | 6 |
|---|---|---|---|---|---|---|
| Total Charges | $45 | $90 | $135 | $180 | $225 | $270 |

b.

| Number of Months | 1 | 2 | 3 | 4 | 5 | 6 |
|---|---|---|---|---|---|---|
| Total Charges | $95 | $140 | $185 | $230 | $275 | $320 |

c.

| Number of Months | 1 | 2 | 3 | 4 | 5 | 6 |
|---|---|---|---|---|---|---|
| Total Charges | $95 | $190 | $285 | $380 | $475 | $570 |

d.

| Number of Months | 1 | 2 | 3 | 4 | 5 | 6 |
|---|---|---|---|---|---|---|
| Total Charges | $50 | $95 | $140 | $185 | $230 | $275 |

10. This table shows bases, heights, and areas of four triangles. In each triangle, the base remains the same and the height changes.

Triangles

| Base, b | 30 yards | 30 yards | 30 yards | 30 yards |
|---|---|---|---|---|
| Height, h | 20 yards | 40 yards | 60 yards | 80 yards |
| Area, A | 300 square yards | 600 square yards | 900 square yards | 1200 square yards |

Which formula best represents the relationship between $A$, the areas of these triangles, and $h$, their heights?

a. $A = \dfrac{h}{30}$

b. $A = \dfrac{h}{15}$

c. $A = 30h$

d. $A = 15h$

11. An automobile mechanic charges $65 per hour when repairing an automobile. There is also a charge for the parts required. Which equation can the mechanic use to calculate the charge, $c$, to repair an automobile which requires $h$ hours and $p$ dollars worth of parts?

    a. $c = 65(h + p)$
    b. $c = 65h + p$
    c. $c = 65p + h$
    d. $c = h + p$

12. Greg knows that in the triangle below, $m\angle X$ is 50° more than $m\angle V$.

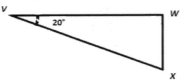

What is the measure of $\angle W$?

    a. 20°
    b. 50°
    c. 70°
    d. 90°

13. There are five points labeled on this grid.

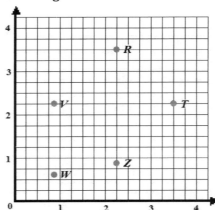

Which of the points on the grid best represents the point at $(3\frac{1}{2}, 2\frac{1}{4})$?

    a. R
    b. T
    c. V
    d. W

14. Curtis measured the temperature of water in a flask in Science class. The temperature of the water was 35°C. He carefully heated the flask so that the temperature of the water increased about 2°C every 3 minutes. Approximately how much had the temperature of the water increased after 20 minutes?

    a. 10°C
    b. 13°C
    c. 15°C
    d. 35°C

15. Carlos helped in the library by putting new books on the shelves. Each shelf held between 21 and 24 books. Each bookcase had 5 shelves and Carlos filled 2 of the bookcases. Which number is nearest to the number of books Carlos put on the shelves?

    a. 100
    b. 195
    c. 215
    d. 240

16. The distance from Miriam's home to her aunt's house is 27 kilometers. What is that distance in meters?

    a. 270 meters
    b. 2,700 meters
    c. 27,000 meters
    d. 27,000,000 meters

17. Jacob recorded the high temperature in his backyard each day for six days. The list below shows those high temperatures.

$$61°, 54°, 58°, 63°, 71°, 71°$$

Which of these temperatures is the median of the ones in Jacob's list?

    a. 17°
    b. 62°
    c. 63°
    d. 71°

18. Mr. Smith paid $60 for a kit to build a dollhouse for his granddaughter. He also paid $10 for tools, $20 for paint, and $10 for other supplies to build the dollhouse. Which graph best represents the dollhouse expenses Mr. Smith had?

a.

c.

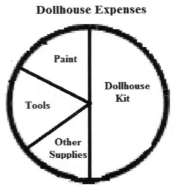

b.

d.

19. People who attended an orchestra concert at Johnson Middle School were asked to which of five age groups they belonged. The data is recorded in this graph.

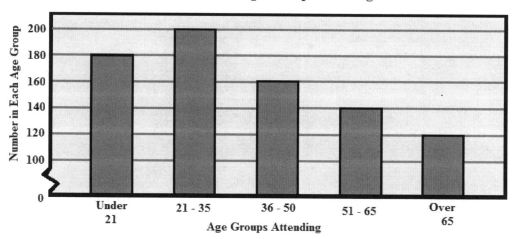

Which table correctly represents the data recorded in the graph?

a.

Number of Each Age Group Attending Concert

| Age Group (in years) | Under 21 | 21 – 35 | 36 – 50 | 51 – 65 | Over 65 |
|---|---|---|---|---|---|
| Number in Group | 180 | 200 | 160 | 140 | 120 |

b.

Number of Each Age Group Attending Concert

| Age Group (in years) | Under 21 | 21 – 35 | 36 – 50 | 51 – 65 | Over 65 |
|---|---|---|---|---|---|
| Number in Group | 180 | 220 | 180 | 160 | 140 |

c.

Number of Each Age Group Attending Concert

| Age Group (in years) | Under 21 | 21 – 35 | 36 – 50 | 51 – 65 | Over 65 |
|---|---|---|---|---|---|
| Number in Group | 180 | 200 | 140 | 120 | 100 |

d.

Number of Each Age Group Attending Concert

| Age Group (in years) | Under 21 | 21 – 35 | 36 – 50 | 51 – 65 | Over 65 |
|---|---|---|---|---|---|
| Number in Group | 180 | 200 | 160 | 120 | 120 |

20. The cashier at Weekender Video Arcade recorded the number of tokens sold on Thursday, Friday, Saturday, and Sunday during one weekend. The graph shows the number of tokens sold on each of those four days.

If the tokens sell for $1, what amount of money should the cashier have received for tokens sold on Friday and Saturday combined?

    a. $500
    b. $800
    c. $1,200
    d. $2,000

21. At the park, a canoe can be rented for $6 for the afternoon. A rowboat can be rented for $8 for the afternoon. The cashier collected a total of $154 one afternoon renting canoes and rowboats. If 15 canoes were rented, how many rowboats were rented that afternoon?

    Place your answer on the provided griddable sheet.

22. Mr. Foster wants to put new carpet on the floor of his rectangular playroom. The playroom is 27 feet long and 18 feet wide. He has found an inexpensive carpet that is priced $14 per square yard. What would be a reasonable price for enough carpet to cover the floor of his playroom?

    a. $486
    b. $756
    c. $1,260
    d. $2,268

23. Tanisha bought 6 new binders for school and paid $4 for each binder. A few days later, she saw the same binders on sale at another store for 2 for $6. How much money could Tanisha have saved if she had bought the binders at the store where they went on sale?

    a. $6
    b. $7
    c. $15
    d. $18

24. Kenneth needs to repaint a wall in his bathroom. The wall is 8 feet high and 14 feet long. Part of the wall is covered with tile and he will not paint that part. The part of the wall covered by tile is 14 feet long and 42 inches high. Which expression could Kenneth use to find the area of the part of the wall he needs to repaint?

 a. $14 \times 8 - (42 + 8)$
 b. $14 \times 8 - (42 \times 14)$
 c. $14 \times 8 - [(42 \div 12) \times 14]$
 d. $2(14 + 8) - [(42 \div 12) + 14]$

25. In a new apartment building being built, it was decided that only numbers that appear in both of the following lists would be given as apartment numbers. Both lists increase arithmetically.

List 1: 2, 5, 8, 11, 14, ...

List 2: 1, 5, 9, 13, 17, ...

Which of the following sets of numbers contain three numbers which can be given as apartment numbers in the new building?

 a. 5, 17, 23
 b. 5, 17, 29
 c. 17, 29, 37
 d. 17, 29, 43

26. Arlene had a garden for flowers. The rectangular garden was 10 feet wide and 16 feet long. In the garden, she planted daisies in a rectangular plot 5 feet wide and 10 feet long. She also planted pansies in a square plot 6 feet on each side. If Arlene planted no other flowers, how much area in her garden could still be planted?

 a. 13 square feet, because $2(10 + 16) - [2(5 + 10) + 2(6 + 6)] = 13$
 b. 38 square feet, because $2(10 + 16) - (5 \times 10) + (6 \times 6) = 38$
 c. 74 square feet, because $10 \times 16 - [(5 \times 10) + (6 \times 6)] = 74$
 d. 146 square feet, because $10 \times 16 - (5 \times 100) + (6 \times 6) = 146$

27. There are five points labeled on this grid.

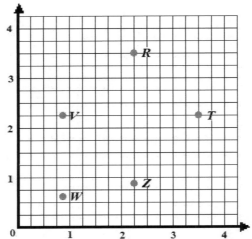

Which of the coordinates on the grid best represents the point R?

a. $(3\frac{1}{2}, 2\frac{1}{2})$

b. $(2\frac{1}{4}, 3\frac{1}{2})$

c. $(3\frac{1}{2}, 4\frac{1}{2})$

d. $(2\frac{1}{4}, 3\frac{1}{4})$

28. The soccer field was 30 yards long. What is that distance in feet?

Place your answer on the provided griddable sheet.

29. Marjorie collected the ages of her friends. What is the range of her friends' ages?

10, 12, 8, 7, 14, 10, 11, 9

Place your answer on the provided griddable answer sheet.

30. Xander was given 10 cups of birdfeed to pour into four birdfeeders. He poured 2 cups of feed into one feeder, 4 cups of feed into the second feeder, 2 cups of feed into the third feeder, and 1 cup into the fourth feeder. He did not put birdfeed anywhere else. Which expression best represents the amount of birdfeed leftover after Xander poured birdfeed into the four birdfeeders?

a. 10 + 2 + 4 + 2 + 1

b. 2 + 4 + 2 + 1 -10

c. 4 – 10 + 2 + 2 +1

d. 10 – 2 – 4 – 2 - 1

- 70 -

31. The relationship between various sets of numbers is shown in the Venn diagram below. To which of the following sets of numbers does the number 0 belong?

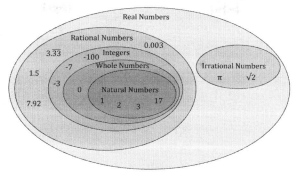

    a. Real numbers and irrational numbers
    b. Real numbers, rational numbers, integers, and whole numbers
    c. Real numbers, rational numbers, integers, whole numbers, and natural numbers
    d. Real numbers, rational numbers, and irrational numbers

32. Given the number 3, what is its opposite and its absolute value?

    a. The opposite of 3 is -3, and the |3| is 3.
    b. The opposite of 3 is -3, and the |3| is -3.
    c. The opposite of 3 is 3, and the |3| is 3.
    d. The opposite of 3 is -3, and the |3| is -3.

33. Which of the following lists of rational numbers is listed in decreasing order?

    a. 22.002, 2.002, 0.00202, 0.222
    b. 0.0002, 0.00202, 0.0202, 0.2002
    c. 2.02, 2.222, 0.22, 0.00002
    d. 2.2, 2.002, 2.0, 0.202

34. Which of the following is equivalent to 24?

    a. $2 \cdot 2 \cdot 3$
    b. $2 \cdot 2 \cdot 2 \cdot 3$
    c. $2 \cdot 2 \cdot 3 \cdot 3$
    d. $2 \cdot 2 \cdot 2 \cdot 2$

35. Which of the following expressions is equivalent to $x + x + x + x \cdot x$?

    a. $x^3 + 2x$
    b. $x^5$
    c. $5x$
    d. $3x + x^2$

36. Which size of tomato sauce shown in the table has the lowest unit price?

| Size (oz) | Cost ($) |
|-----------|----------|
| 8 | $1.80 |
| 16 | $2.99 |
| 24 | $4.19 |
| 32 | $8.40 |

a. 8 oz
b. 16 oz
c. 24 oz
d. 32 oz

37. Which vehicle shown in the table has the slowest speed?

| Vehicle | Time (hr) | Distance (mi) |
|---------|-----------|---------------|
| Car | 4 | 180 |
| Truck | 6 | 360 |
| Motorcycle | 1.5 | 85.2 |
| Minivan | 2.5 | 162.5 |

a. Car
b. Truck
c. Motorcycle
d. Minivan

38. Which of the following statements is true about the relationship represented by the table below?

| x | y |
|---|---|
| 0 | 0 |
| 3 | 12 |
| 6 | 24 |
| 9 | 36 |

a. The dependent variable is $x$.
b. The independent variable is $y$.
c. As $x$ increases, $y$ increases.
d. The value of $y$ is independent of the value of $x$.

39. Which of the following equations is equivalent to this verbal description?

Maxine is five years older than her brother Ivan.

a. $y = x + 5$
b. $y = 5$
c. $y = 5x$
d. $x + y = 5$

40. Which of the following equations represents the graph shown below?

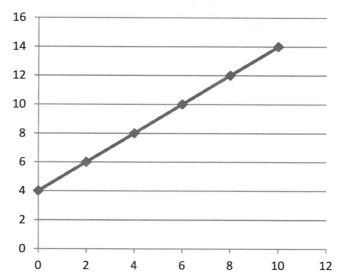

a. $y = x + 1$
b. $y = x + 4$
c. $y = x + 3$
d. $y = x + 2$

41. Which of the following sets of ordered pairs corresponds to this verbal description?
The cost of coffee is 2.50 times the number of pounds of coffee.

a. (0, 0), (2, 2.50), (4, 5.00), (6, 10.00)
b. (0, 2.50), (1, 5.00), (2, 7.50), (3, 10.00)
c. (0, 0), (1, 5.00), (2, 10.00), (3, 15.00)
d. (0, 0), (2, 5.00), (4, 10.00), (6, 15.00)

42. Which of the following equations represents this situation?
Mandy is six years older than Courtney. If Mandy is fourteen years old, how old is Courtney?

a. $6 = x + 14$
b. $14 + 6 = x$
c. $14 = x + 6$
d. $14 = 6x$

- 73 -

43. Which of the following is the correct representation for the solution of $3x \geq 6$?

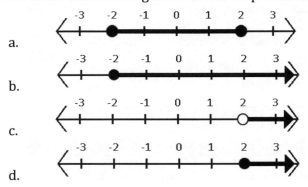

a.

b.

c.

d.

44. Which of the following real-world situations is best represented by $x - 5 > 7$?

a. If Sondra chews five of her pieces of gum, she still will have more than seven pieces of gum.
b. If Katrina eats seven of her donuts, she still will have fewer than five donuts left.
c. If Lucas gains five more bonus points, he will have more than seven bonus points.
d. If Dakota sells seven comedies from his movie collection, he will have no more than five movies left.

45. Which of the following values makes the given equation true?

a. $22 - x = 14; \; x = 9$
b. $7 + x = 35; \; x = 26$
c. $30 = 43 - x; \; x = 13$
d. $x + 103 = 214; \; x = 110$

46. Which of the following values makes the given inequality true?

a. $x - 12 < 15; \; x = 30$
b. $x + 33 > 67; \; x = 32$
c. $12x < 77; \; x = 6$
d. $21x > 100; \; x = 4$

47. Mr. Richter lists his 6th grade math test scores below. What are the median and mode for this data?

$$77, 88, 98, 77, 77, 88, 91, 98, 96, 96, 94, 92, 84, 80, 75$$

a. Median = 87.4; Mode = 88
b. Median = 77; Mode = 88
c. Median = 87.4; Mode = 77
d. Median = 88; Mode = 77

48. Sally surveys her friends to determine the number of texts they receive each day and lists the data below. What is the interquartile range (IQR) for this data?

$$22, 50, 44, 66, 38, 109, 56, 17, 47, 33, 35$$

a. 23
b. 44
c. 92
d. 27

- 74 -

49. What is the mean of the data below?

| Stem | Leaf |
|------|------|
| 1 | 2 4 4 |
| 2 | 1 4 |
| 3 | 2 |
| 4 | 1 2 |

    a. 25
    b. 20
    c. 27
    d. 23

50. Which of the following is NOT true regarding credit reports?
    a. A higher credit score indicates a higher risk to the lender in terms of the loan being repaid.
    b. Borrowers can raise their credit scores by paying off debt.
    c. Borrowers with higher credit scores are more likely to receive approvals for their loans.
    d. Credit reports enable borrowers to know how they are viewed by potential lenders.

51. Which of the following methods of paying for college are awarded based on financial need and do not need to be repaid unless a student withdraws from school?
    a. Student loan
    b. Scholarships
    c. Grants
    d. Savings

52. Which of the following methods of paying for college is actually a part-time job provided by the college that enables the student to work on campus to earn money to pay for college?
    a. Grant
    b. Student loan
    c. Scholarship
    d. Work-study

53. What is the balance of this check register after the transaction on 3/17?

| Number or code | Date | Description of transaction | Withdrawal/ Payment/Fee (-) | | Deposit/ Credit (+) | | Balance | |
|---|---|---|---|---|---|---|---|---|
| | 2/12 | | | | | | 500 | 36 |
| 135 | 2/14 | Pizza Planet | 25 | 17 | | | | |
| | 2/22 | ATM withdrawal from my bank | 40 | 00 | | | | |
| | 3/13 | Online payment to movie service | 7 | 99 | | | | |
| | 3/15 | Deposit of birthday money | | | 85 | 00 | | |
| | 3/16 | Deposit from moving job | | | 45 | 00 | | |
| | 3/17 | Transfer to savings | 175 | 00 | | | | |
| | | | | | | | | |

a. $212.20
b. $382.20
c. $292.20
d. $432.54

54. Matthew is researching typical average annual incomes for potential careers. Which of the following careers has a 30-year income over $2,000,000?

| Career | | Average Income |
|---|---|---|
| Personal trainer | | $48,000 |
| Mechanical Engineer | | $72,000 |
| Computer Programmer | | $64,000 |
| Math teacher | | $58,000 |

a. Mechanical engineer and computer programmer
b. Only a mechanical engineer
c. Mechanical engineer, computer programmer, and math teacher
d. None of these careers

55. One morning at Jim's café, 25 people ordered juice, 10 ordered milk, and 50 ordered coffee with breakfast. Which ratio best compares the number of people who ordered milk to the number of people who ordered juice?

a. 5 to 7
b. 5 to 2
c. 2 to 7
d. 2 to 5

56. At the middle school Vanessa attends, there are 240 Grade 6 students, 210 Grade 7 students, and 200 Grade 8 students. Which ratio best compares the number of students in Grade 8 to the number of students in Grade 6 at Vanessa's school?

a. 5 : 6
b. 5 : 11
c. 6 : 5
d. 7 : 8

# Answers and Explanations

## TEKS Standard (6.2)(D)

**1. D:** To correctly order the numbers in this question, making the decimals all have the same number of digits by adding as many zeros as necessary to the numbers with fewer digits makes them easier to compare. Here, only 17.4 has fewer digits than the others, so add one zero to make it 17.40 (*this does not change the value*). Now, by comparing place values from left to right of 17.03, 17.4, 17.31, and 17.09, we see that 17.03 is the shortest, 17.09 is the next longest, 17.31 is the third longest, and 17.4 is the longest. Notice the question asked for shortest to longest, not longest to shortest.

## TEKS Standard (6.4)(E)

**2. A:** In order to answer this question, we add the number of baseball and football cards to realize that there are 50 total cards in Castor's collection, 40 of which are baseball cards. To convert this to a decimal, we need to divide 40 by 50. This gives the correct answer, 0.8.

## TEKS Standard (6.7)(A)

**3. C:** There is more than one way to solve this problem. One method is to use the fact that the number ends in 0. This means 10 is a factor. So, $10 \times 63 = 630$. 10 has prime factors of 2 and 5. 63 has factors of 7 and 9 and the 9 has two factors of 3. Putting the prime factors in order, least to greatest, and showing the two factors of 3 with an exponent of 2 gives us the answer: $2 \times 3^2 \times 5 \times 7$.

## TEKS Standard (6.7)(A)

**4. B:** There is more than one way to solve this problem. One method is to find the least common multiple of 60 and 80. To do this, first find the prime factors of each number.

$60 = 2 \times 2 \times 3 \times 5$

$80 = 2 \times 2 \times 2 \times 2 \times 5$

The factors common to 60 and 80 are 2, 2, and 5. The factors that are not common to both numbers are two factors of 2 from 80 and a factor of 3 from 60. To find the least common multiple, multiply all the factors without repetition. That is, multiply the common factors (2, 2, and 5) and the other factors (2, 2, and 3) together:

$2 \times 2 \times 2 \times 2 \times 3 \times 5 = 240$

240 is the least common multiple. This is the total number of beads needed of each color. To find how many bags the club will need to purchase, divide this total by the number of beads that come in each bag for each color bead. $240 \div 60 = 4$ (4 bags of blue). $240 \div 80 = 3$ (3 bags of silver).

## TEKS Standard (6.4)(C)

**5. C:** The ratio compares the number of coffee drinkers to the number of tea drinkers, in that order, so the ratio is 45 to 20. Note that the ratio of 20 to 45 would be incorrect. The ratio of 45 to 20 can then be written in simpler terms by dividing both terms by 5 to get 9 to 4. Notice that the number of hot chocolate drinkers is not important in this problem.

## TEKS Standard (6.4)(G)

**6. C:** The 80% means 80 out of 100, which can be written as $\frac{80}{100}$. This fraction can be written in lowest terms by dividing both the numerator and denominator by the greatest common factor of 20, to get the fraction, $\frac{4}{5}$.

### TEKS Standard (6.4)(F)

**7. D:** The number of shaded parts is 8 and the total number of parts is 10. This can be written as the ratio: $\frac{8}{10}$. Since percent is always a ratio with a denominator of 100, multiply both terms of the ratio by 10 to get the ratio: $\frac{80}{100}$, which can be written as 80%.

### TEKS Standard (6.4)(C)

**8. B:** One method that can be used to answer this question is to write and solve the proportion: $\frac{3}{20} = \frac{V}{360}$, where $V$ stands for the number of Brand V televisions that were sold at the furniture store. To solve the proportion, we can cross multiply: 20 times $V$ and 3 times 360, which gives the equation: $20V = 1,080$. We solve this equation by dividing both sides of the equation by 20 to get $V = 54$.

### TEKS Standard (6.3)(D)

**9. B:** There is a one-time charge of $50 for the price of the phone and a $45 monthly charge in the first month for a total of $95. Then, a charge of $45 only is added for every month after that. Since the chart shows the total charge each month, adding $45 to the total due from the first month gives a total of $140 for the first 2 months. Then, $45 is added for the next month, for a total of $185 for the first 3 months, $230 for 4 months, $275 for 5 months, and $320 in total charges for the first 6 months.

### TEKS Standard (6.8)(C)

**10. D:** The formula for the area of a triangle can be used here, but it is not necessary. To find the relationship between the heights and areas, look at the last two rows. A pattern can be seen that each value for the area, $A$, is just 15 times the value of the height, $h$. So, the formula is: $A = 15h$.

### TEKS Standard (6.9)(A)

**11. B:** The amount charged for hours worked will require us to multiply the number of hours by $65. The charge for parts is not changed by the number of hours worked. So, the equation needs to show 65 times $h$, the number of hours, plus $p$, the price of the parts. So, the correct equation is: $c = 65h + p$.

### TEKS Standard (6.8)(A)

**12. D:** To find $m\angle W$, we must first find the measure of $\angle X$. We know $m\angle X$ is 50° more than $m\angle V$. Since $m\angle V = 20°$, then $m\angle X = 20° + 50° = 70°$. So, $m\angle V + m\angle X = 90°$. It is important here to know that the sum of the three angles of any triangle is 180°. Since $m\angle V + m\angle X = 90°$, then $90° + m\angle W = 180°$. So, $m\angle W = 90°$.

### TEKS Standard (6.11)(A)

- 78 -

**13. B:** Each of the units represents $\frac{1}{4}$. The point $T$ is 14 units right of the $y$-axis or $\frac{14}{4}$ units, which is equivalent to $3\frac{1}{2}$. The point $T$ is also 9 units from the $x$-axis, or $\frac{9}{4}$, which is equivalent to $2\frac{1}{4}$. Be careful to notice that coordinate pairs always come in the order of the $x$-coordinate and then the $y$-coordinate, which is why Point $R$ would be incorrect.

### TEKS Standard (6.3)(D)

**14. B:** The water temperature increased by about 2° every 3 minutes, or $\frac{2}{3}$ of a degree every minute. Multiplying the increase in degrees per minute by the total number of minutes yields

$$\frac{2°}{3 \text{ min}} \times 20 \text{ min} = \frac{40}{3}, \text{ or } 13.33°$$

Since the problem asks for the increase in temperature and not the total temperature that results after the increases, 13 is the closest to our answer.

### TEKS Standard (6.3)(D)

**15. C:** First, since there are 5 shelves on each of the 2 bookcases, we multiply 5 by 2 to get 10 shelves total. Then, we find the minimum and maximum number of books that could have filled the shelves. Since 21 times 10 is 210 and 24 times 10 is 240, The number of books he shelved must be between 210 and 240. Answer D is 240, which would mean that every shelf was filled with the maximum number of books, which is not as likely.

### TEKS Standard (6.4)(H)

**16. C:** There are 1,000 meters in every kilometer. Since we are converting from a larger unit to a smaller unit, we should multiply the number of the larger unit by the conversion factor. That gives us 27 times 1,000, which equals 27,000.

### TEKS Standard (6.12)(C)

**17. B:** To find the median of a set of data, first arrange the numbers in numerical order. Since this is an even numbered list, the two most central numbers are 61 and 63. Midway between these numbers is 62.

### TEKS Standard (6.12)(A)

**18. D:** By adding up all of Mr. Smith's expenses for the dollhouse, $60 + $10 + $20 + $10, you find that his expenses totaled $100. Mr. Smith spent $60 on the kit, which is more than $\frac{1}{2}$ his expenses ($\frac{1}{2}$ of $100 would be $50), $\frac{1}{10}$ of his expenses on tools ($\frac{1}{10}$ of $100 = $10), $\frac{1}{5}$ of his expenses on paint ($\frac{1}{5}$ of $100 = $20), and $\frac{1}{10}$ of his expenses on other supplies. This is the only graph that correctly shows these fractions.

### TEKS Standard (6.12)(A)

**19. A:** This table is the only one with the correct numbers from the graph for each category.

### TEKS Standard (6.13)(A)

**20. D:** Though the graph shows the numbers of tokens sold on Thursday through Sunday, we are only asked about those sold on Friday and Saturday. So, we add those numbers together to get 800

+ 1,200 = 2,000. Then, since each of the 2,000 tokens sold for $1 each, the 2,000 should be multiplied by $1 to get $2000.

## TEKS Standard (6.3)(D)

**21. 8:** To find the answer to this question, first find the total amount of money spent to rent 15 canoes. Multiply 15 times $6 to get $90. The remainder of the $154 that was spent on both canoes and rowboats is the amount spent on rowboats, so $154 – $90 is $64. Then we divide $64 by $8 (the price to rent a rowboat) to get 8, which is the number of rowboats rented.

## TEKS Standard (6.8)(D)

**22. B:** It is necessary to find the area of the floor by multiplying the dimensions together. However, since the dimensions are given in feet and we only know the price of carpeting per square yard, converting the dimensions from feet to yards first is helpful. Since there are 3 feet in a yard, dividing each of the dimensions by 3 will give us the measurements in yards. So, 18/3 = 6 and 27/3 = 9. So, the floor is 6 yards by 9 yards, which is an area of 54 square yards. Last, we multiply 54 by $14, since each square yard costs $14 and there are 54, so the price of the carpet should be $756.

## TEKS Standard (6.3)(D)

**23. A:** To find the answer, first determine the amount the binders cost at the different stores. At the first store, the price would be 6 times $4, since each binder costs $4, which is $24. At the second store, the binders are sold in twos. 6 binders would be 3 pairs of binders, and since each pair costs $6, $6 times 3 is the total cost of the binders at the second store, which is $18. We then subtract to find the difference, $24 - $18 = $6.

## TEKS Standard (6.8)(C)

**24. C:** We multiply the length and wide of the wall to find the area of the entire wall. So, 8 × 14. Then, we want to subtract the area of the tiled section that does not need to be painted from the area of the entire wall. However, the height of the tiled section is given in inches, while all the other dimensions in the problem are given in feet. So, we must convert this to feet. Since we are going from a smaller unit to a larger unit (inches to feet), we want to divide. We need to divide 42 by 12 since that is the conversion factor (12 inches in 1 foot). Then we multiply the height (in feet) by the length to find the area covered by the tile. So, this is 14 times the 42 divided by 12. Last, we subtract the two areas to find the area of the part of the wall Kenneth will repaint.

## TEKS Standard (6.2)(D)

**25. B:** Since the first list increases by 3's and the second list by 4's, this means that the apartment numbers together increase by 12's (3 times 4). Since the two lists begin at different values, it is important to note that 5 is the first apartment number the two lists have in common. So, the set of numbers which can be apartment numbers can be found by increasing arithmetically by 12 starting at 5: 5, 17, 29, 41, 53, 65, .... The numbers 5, 17, and 29 are all in both lists.

## TEKS Standard (6.8)(D)

**26. C:** The area of the garden should be found by multiplying 10 times 16 to get 160. Then the area of the daisy plot can be found by multiplying 5 times 10 to get 50, and the area of the pansy plot can be found by multiplying 6 times 6 to get 36. We then add the 50 square feet and 36 square feet to get 86 square feet, which is the area the two plots (daisy and pansy) cover. To find the area of the garden that can still be planted, subtract that from the total area of 160 square feet to get 74 square feet.

## TEKS Standard (6.11)(A)

**27. B:** Each of the units represents $\frac{1}{4}$. The point R is 9 units to the right of the *y*-axis or $\frac{9}{4}$, which is equivalent to $2\frac{1}{4}$. Point R is also 14 units above the *x*-axis or $\frac{14}{4}$, which is equivalent to $3\frac{1}{2}$. Be careful to notice that coordinate pairs always come in the order of the *x*-coordinate and then the *y*-coordinate.

## TEKS Standard (6.4)(H)

**28. 90:** There are 3 feet in every yard; therefore this is a simple multiplication problem. 30 yards X 3 feet/yard = 90 feet.

## TEKS Standard (6.12)(C)

**29. 7:** Begin by arranging the different ages from least to greatest:

7, 8, 9, 10, 10, 11, 12, 14

Range is the difference between the highest and lowest values in a set of data; therefore, 14 − 7 = 7.

## TEKS Standard (6.3)(D)

**30. D:** Only answer D correctly shows each amount of birdfeed being subtracted from the original total amount of 10 cups that originally given to Xander.

## TEKS Standard (6.2)(A)

**31. B:** Real numbers are either rational numbers or irrational numbers. Rational numbers include integers. Integers include whole numbers. Whole numbers include natural numbers. The number 0 is a whole number, integer, rational number, and real number. It is not a natural number or an irrational number. Therefore, choice B is correct.

## TEKS Standard (6.2)(C)

**32. A:** A number and its opposite are equidistant from the number 0 on a number line. The opposite of 3 is -3. The absolute value of a number is its distance from the number 0 on a number line. The |3| is 3. Therefore, choice A is correct.

## TEKS Standard (6.2)(D)

**33. D:** These rational numbers are all decimals. Decimals can be ordered from greatest to least by comparing the digits in each place value. Choice A is incorrect because 0.222 is greater than 0.00202. Choice B is incorrect because the numbers are listed in increasing order. Choice C is incorrect because 2.222 is greater than 2.02. Therefore, choice D is correct.

## TEKS Standard (6.7)(A)

**34. B:** The prime factorization of 24 can be found by splitting 24 into factors such as 4 · 6 and then further splitting these factors into factors consisting only of prime numbers: 2 · 2 · 2 · 3. Therefore, choice B is correct.

- 81 -

## TEKS Standard (6.7)(B)

**35. D:** The $x \cdot x$ can be represented by $x^2$. The $x + x + x$ can be represented by $3x$. So, $x + x + x + x \cdot x$ is equivalent to $3x + x^2$. Therefore, choice D is correct.

## TEKS Standard (6.4)(B)

**36. C:** The unit price for each size is determined by dividing the cost by the number of ounces. For 8 ounces, the unit rate is \$1.89/8 or \$0.23/oz. For 16 ounces, the unit rate is \$2.99/16 or \$0.19/oz. For 24 ounces, the unit rate is \$4.19/24 or \$0.17/oz. For 32 ounces, the unit rate is \$8.40/32 or \$0.26/oz. Therefore, choice C is correct.

## TEKS Standard (6.4)(B)

**37. A:** The speed of each vehicle is determined by dividing the distance by the time. The car travels at 180/4 or 45 mph. The truck travels at 360/6 or 60 mph. The motorcycle travels at 85.2/1.5 or 56.8 mph. The minivan travels at 162.5/2.5 or 65 mph. Therefore, choice A is correct.

## TEKS Standard (6.6)(A)

**38. C:** The independent variable is $x$. The dependent variable is $y$. The value of $y$ depends on the value of $x$. As $x$ increases, $y$ increases. Therefore, choice C is correct.

## TEKS Standard (6.6)(B)

**39. A:** This is an additive relationship. At each age of Ivan, whether he is 10, 16, 27, or older, Maxine is always five years older. If we represent Ivan's age with $x$, then Maxine's age is always $y = x + 5$. Therefore, choice A is correct.

## TEKS Standard (6.6)(C)

**40. B:** The equation can be determined from the ordered pairs associated with the graph. Ordered pairs include (0, 4), (2, 6), (4, 8), (6, 10), (8, 12), and (10, 14). Each $y$-value results from 4 being added to the $x$-value. Therefore, choice B is correct.

## TEKS Standard (6.6)(C)

**41. D:** The equation corresponding to the verbal description can be written as $y = 2.50x$. Then, when $x = 0, y = 0$. When $x = 1, y = 2.50$. When $x = 2, y = 5.00$. When $x = 4, y = 10.00$. When $x = 6, y = 15.00$. Therefore, choice D is correct.

## TEKS Standard (6.9)(A)

**42. C:** Let $x$ represent Courtney's age. Then, since Mandy is six years older than Courtney, 6 is added to $x$. Since Mandy is fourteen years old, $14 = x + 6$. Therefore, choice C is correct.

## TEKS Standard (6.9)(A

**43. D:** The inequality $3x \geq 6$ can be solved by dividing both sides by 3. This results in $x \geq 2$. This solution can be represented with a solid circle at 2 and an arrow to the right. Therefore, choice D is correct.

## TEKS Standard (6.9)(C)

**44. A:** If we think of $x$ as being a quantity of items, then the "minus 5" means that five of those items have been somehow removed. Then, $x - 5 > 7$ means that the difference of the original quantity and five is greater than seven. The scenario that fits is "If Sondra chews five of her pieces of gum, she still will have more than seven left." Therefore, choice A is correct.

### TEKS Standard (6.10)(A)

**45. C:** Since $22 - 9 \neq 14$, choice A is incorrect. Since $7 + 26 \neq 36$, choice B is incorrect. Since $30 = 43 - 13$, choice C is correct. Since $110 + 103 \neq 214$, choice D is incorrect. Therefore, choice C is correct.

### TEKS Standard (6.10)(B)

**46. C:** In option A, 30 – 12 is 18, which is greater than 15, not less than 15. In option B, 32 + 33 is 65, which is less than 67, not greater than 67. In option D, 21(4) is 84, which is less than 100, not greater than 100. However, in option C, 12(6) is 72, which is less than 77. Therefore, choice C is correct.

### TEKS Standard (6.12)(B)

**47. D:** Rank the data from least to greatest: 75, 77, 77, 77, 80, 84, 88, 88, 91, 92, 94, 96, 96, 98, 98. Since there are add odd number of entries, the median is the entry located at the middle of the ranked list; the median is 88. The mode is the entry which occurs most often, namely 77. The mean is the average of the data, or 87.4. Therefore, choice D is correct.

### TEKS Standard (6.12)(C)

**48. A:** Rank the data from least to greatest: 17, 22, 33, 35, 38, 44, 47, 50, 56, 66, 109. Quartile 2 is 44, the median of the data. Quartile 1 is 33, the median of the lower half of the ranked data. Quartile 3 is 56, the median of the upper half of the ranked data. The interquartile range is the difference between Quartile 3 and Quartile 1. Since IQR = $Q_3 - Q_1$, IQR = 56 – 33, or 23. Therefore, choice A is correct.

### TEKS Standard (6.13)(A)

**49. A:** The mean is the average of the data. The average is found by dividing the sum of the data by the number of data points. The average is $\frac{12+14+14+21+24+32+41+42}{8}$, or $\frac{200}{8}$, which is 25. Therefore, choice A is correct.

### TEKS Standard (6.14)(E)

**50. A:** Credit scores range between 300 and 850. The higher the score, the lower the risk is to the lender in terms of the loan being repaid. Therefore, choice A is correct.

### TEKS Standard (6.14)(G)

**51. C:** Scholarships are awarded on merit and do not need to be repaid. Savings are the contribution from the student and the parents towards college expenses. Student loans are loans that must be paid back with interest. Grants are awarded based on a student's financial need and do not need to be repaid unless the student withdrawals from school. Therefore, choice C is correct.

### TEKS Standard (6.14)(G)

**52. D:** Grants and scholarships provide money to the student based on financial need or merit and do not require a student to work on campus. Student loans are loans the student receives and pays back after finishing college. Work-study is a part-time job provided by the college that enables the student to work on campus to earn money to pay for college. Therefore, choice D is correct.

### TEKS Standard (6.14)(C)

**53. B:** Deposits are added to the balance. Withdrawals are subtracted from the balance. The check register is completed below. The account balance after the transaction on 3/17 is $382.20; therefore, choice B is correct. 4.6.14

| Number or code | Date | Description of transaction | Withdrawal/ Payment/Fee (-) | | Deposit/ Credit (+) | | Balance | |
|---|---|---|---|---|---|---|---|---|
| | 2/12 | | | | | | 500 | 36 |
| 135 | 2/14 | Pizza Planet | 25 | 17 | | | 475 | 19 |
| | 2/22 | ATM withdrawal from my bank | 40 | 00 | | | 435 | 19 |
| | 3/13 | Online payment to movie service | 7 | 99 | | | 427 | 20 |
| | 3/15 | Deposit of birthday money | | | 85 | 00 | 512 | 20 |
| | 3/16 | Deposit from moving job | | | 45 | 00 | 557 | 20 |
| | 3/17 | Transfer to savings | 175 | 00 | | | 382 | 20 |
| | | | | | | | | |

### TEKS Standard (6.14)(H)

**54. B:** The 30-year income is calculated by multiplying the average annual income by 30 years. The 30-year incomes for the jobs Matthew is researching are shown below. Of these career choices, only the mechanical engineer has the potential to earn more than $2,000,000. Therefore, choice B is correct. 4.6.14

| Career | Average Income | Lifetime Income |
|---|---|---|
| Personal trainer | $48,000 | $1,440,000 |
| Mechanical Engineer | $72,000 | $2,160,000 |
| Computer Programmer | $64,000 | $1,920,000 |
| Math teacher | $58,000 | $1,740,000 |

### TEKS Standard (6.5)(A)

**55. D:** Note that the ratio asked for is the number of people who ordered milk to the number who ordered juice. The number of people who ordered coffee does not matter here. This compares 10 to 25, and the order is important here. Since the ratio is with the number of people who ordered milk first, the 10 must come first. So, the ratio is 10 to 25, but the ratio can be written in simpler form by dividing both numbers in the ratio by 5, to get the ratio: 2 to 5.

**56. A:** One way to answer this question is to name the ratio: 200 to 240, then write the ratio in simplest terms by dividing both terms by the greatest common factor, 40, to get 5 to 6. It should be noted that the number of Grade 7 students is not important for this problem. Also, the order of the ratio matters. Since it asks for the ratio using the number of Grade 8 students first, the ratio is 200 to 240 and not the other way around.

# How to Overcome Test Anxiety

Just the thought of taking a test is enough to make most people a little nervous. A test is an important event that can have a long-term impact on your future, so it's important to take it seriously and it's natural to feel anxious about performing well. But just because anxiety is normal, that doesn't mean that it's helpful in test taking, or that you should simply accept it as part of your life. Anxiety can have a variety of effects. These effects can be mild, like making you feel slightly nervous, or severe, like blocking your ability to focus or remember even a simple detail.

If you experience test anxiety—whether severe or mild—it's important to know how to beat it. To discover this, first you need to understand what causes test anxiety.

## Causes of Test Anxiety

While we often think of anxiety as an uncontrollable emotional state, it can actually be caused by simple, practical things. One of the most common causes of test anxiety is that a person does not feel adequately prepared for their test. This feeling can be the result of many different issues such as poor study habits or lack of organization, but the most common culprit is time management. Starting to study too late, failing to organize your study time to cover all of the material, or being distracted while you study will mean that you're not well prepared for the test. This may lead to cramming the night before, which will cause you to be physically and mentally exhausted for the test. Poor time management also contributes to feelings of stress, fear, and hopelessness as you realize you are not well prepared but don't know what to do about it.

Other times, test anxiety is not related to your preparation for the test but comes from unresolved fear. This may be a past failure on a test, or poor performance on tests in general. It may come from comparing yourself to others who seem to be performing better or from the stress of living up to expectations. Anxiety may be driven by fears of the future—how failure on this test would affect your educational and career goals. These fears are often completely irrational, but they can still negatively impact your test performance.

> **Review Video: 3 Reasons You Have Test Anxiety**
> Visit mometrix.com/academy and enter code: 428468

# Elements of Test Anxiety

As mentioned earlier, test anxiety is considered to be an emotional state, but it has physical and mental components as well. Sometimes you may not even realize that you are suffering from test anxiety until you notice the physical symptoms. These can include trembling hands, rapid heartbeat, sweating, nausea, and tense muscles. Extreme anxiety may lead to fainting or vomiting. Obviously, any of these symptoms can have a negative impact on testing. It is important to recognize them as soon as they begin to occur so that you can address the problem before it damages your performance.

> **Review Video:** 3 Ways to Tell You Have Test Anxiety
> Visit mometrix.com/academy and enter code: 927847

The mental components of test anxiety include trouble focusing and inability to remember learned information. During a test, your mind is on high alert, which can help you recall information and stay focused for an extended period of time. However, anxiety interferes with your mind's natural processes, causing you to blank out, even on the questions you know well. The strain of testing during anxiety makes it difficult to stay focused, especially on a test that may take several hours. Extreme anxiety can take a huge mental toll, making it difficult not only to recall test information but even to understand the test questions or pull your thoughts together.

> **Review Video:** How Test Anxiety Affects Memory
> Visit mometrix.com/academy and enter code: 609003

# Effects of Test Anxiety

Test anxiety is like a disease—if left untreated, it will get progressively worse. Anxiety leads to poor performance, and this reinforces the feelings of fear and failure, which in turn lead to poor performances on subsequent tests. It can grow from a mild nervousness to a crippling condition. If allowed to progress, test anxiety can have a big impact on your schooling, and consequently on your future.

Test anxiety can spread to other parts of your life. Anxiety on tests can become anxiety in any stressful situation, and blanking on a test can turn into panicking in a job situation. But fortunately, you don't have to let anxiety rule your testing and determine your grades. There are a number of relatively simple steps you can take to move past anxiety and function normally on a test and in the rest of life.

> **Review Video:** How Test Anxiety Impacts Your Grades
> Visit mometrix.com/academy and enter code: 939819

# Physical Steps for Beating Test Anxiety

While test anxiety is a serious problem, the good news is that it can be overcome. It doesn't have to control your ability to think and remember information. While it may take time, you can begin taking steps today to beat anxiety.

Just as your first hint that you may be struggling with anxiety comes from the physical symptoms, the first step to treating it is also physical. Rest is crucial for having a clear, strong mind. If you are tired, it is much easier to give in to anxiety. But if you establish good sleep habits, your body and mind will be ready to perform optimally, without the strain of exhaustion. Additionally, sleeping well helps you to retain information better, so you're more likely to recall the answers when you see the test questions.

Getting good sleep means more than going to bed on time. It's important to allow your brain time to relax. Take study breaks from time to time so it doesn't get overworked, and don't study right before bed. Take time to rest your mind before trying to rest your body, or you may find it difficult to fall asleep.

> **Review Video: The Importance of Sleep for Your Brain**
> Visit mometrix.com/academy and enter code: 319338

Along with sleep, other aspects of physical health are important in preparing for a test. Good nutrition is vital for good brain function. Sugary foods and drinks may give a burst of energy but this burst is followed by a crash, both physically and emotionally. Instead, fuel your body with protein and vitamin-rich foods.

Also, drink plenty of water. Dehydration can lead to headaches and exhaustion, especially if your brain is already under stress from the rigors of the test. Particularly if your test is a long one, drink water during the breaks. And if possible, take an energy-boosting snack to eat between sections.

> **Review Video: How Diet Can Affect your Mood**
> Visit mometrix.com/academy and enter code: 624317

Along with sleep and diet, a third important part of physical health is exercise. Maintaining a steady workout schedule is helpful, but even taking 5-minute study breaks to walk can help get your blood pumping faster and clear your head. Exercise also releases endorphins, which contribute to a positive feeling and can help combat test anxiety.

When you nurture your physical health, you are also contributing to your mental health. If your body is healthy, your mind is much more likely to be healthy as well. So take time to rest, nourish your body with healthy food and water, and get moving as much as possible. Taking these physical steps will make you stronger and more able to take the mental steps necessary to overcome test anxiety.

> **Review Video: How to Stay Healthy and Prevent Test Anxiety**
> Visit mometrix.com/academy and enter code: 877894

# Mental Steps for Beating Test Anxiety

Working on the mental side of test anxiety can be more challenging, but as with the physical side, there are clear steps you can take to overcome it. As mentioned earlier, test anxiety often stems from lack of preparation, so the obvious solution is to prepare for the test. Effective studying may be the most important weapon you have for beating test anxiety, but you can and should employ several other mental tools to combat fear.

First, boost your confidence by reminding yourself of past success—tests or projects that you aced. If you're putting as much effort into preparing for this test as you did for those, there's no reason you should expect to fail here. Work hard to prepare; then trust your preparation.

Second, surround yourself with encouraging people. It can be helpful to find a study group, but be sure that the people you're around will encourage a positive attitude. If you spend time with others who are anxious or cynical, this will only contribute to your own anxiety. Look for others who are motivated to study hard from a desire to succeed, not from a fear of failure.

Third, reward yourself. A test is physically and mentally tiring, even without anxiety, and it can be helpful to have something to look forward to. Plan an activity following the test, regardless of the outcome, such as going to a movie or getting ice cream.

When you are taking the test, if you find yourself beginning to feel anxious, remind yourself that you know the material. Visualize successfully completing the test. Then take a few deep, relaxing breaths and return to it. Work through the questions carefully but with confidence, knowing that you are capable of succeeding.

Developing a healthy mental approach to test taking will also aid in other areas of life. Test anxiety affects more than just the actual test—it can be damaging to your mental health and even contribute to depression. It's important to beat test anxiety before it becomes a problem for more than testing.

> **Review Video: Test Anxiety and Depression**
> Visit mometrix.com/academy and enter code: 904704

# Study Strategy

Being prepared for the test is necessary to combat anxiety, but what does being prepared look like? You may study for hours on end and still not feel prepared. What you need is a strategy for test prep. The next few pages outline our recommended steps to help you plan out and conquer the challenge of preparation.

## Step 1: Scope Out the Test

Learn everything you can about the format (multiple choice, essay, etc.) and what will be on the test. Gather any study materials, course outlines, or sample exams that may be available. Not only will this help you to prepare, but knowing what to expect can help to alleviate test anxiety.

## Step 2: Map Out the Material

Look through the textbook or study guide and make note of how many chapters or sections it has. Then divide these over the time you have. For example, if a book has 15 chapters and you have five days to study, you need to cover three chapters each day. Even better, if you have the time, leave an extra day at the end for overall review after you have gone through the material in depth.

If time is limited, you may need to prioritize the material. Look through it and make note of which sections you think you already have a good grasp on, and which need review. While you are studying, skim quickly through the familiar sections and take more time on the challenging parts. Write out your plan so you don't get lost as you go. Having a written plan also helps you feel more in control of the study, so anxiety is less likely to arise from feeling overwhelmed at the amount to cover. A sample plan may look like this:

- Day 1: Skim chapters 1–4, study chapter 5 (especially pages 31–33)
- Day 2: Study chapters 6–7, skim chapters 8–9
- Day 3: Skim chapter 10, study chapters 11–12 (especially pages 87–90)
- Day 4: Study chapters 13–15
- Day 5: Overall review (focus most on chapters 5, 6, and 12), take practice test

## Step 3: Gather Your Tools

Decide what study method works best for you. Do you prefer to highlight in the book as you study and then go back over the highlighted portions? Or do you type out notes of the important information? Or is it helpful to make flashcards that you can carry with you? Assemble the pens, index cards, highlighters, post-it notes, and any other materials you may need so you won't be distracted by getting up to find things while you study.

If you're having a hard time retaining the information or organizing your notes, experiment with different methods. For example, try color-coding by subject with colored pens, highlighters, or post-it notes. If you learn better by hearing, try recording yourself reading your notes so you can listen while in the car, working out, or simply sitting at your desk. Ask a friend to quiz you from your flashcards, or try teaching someone the material to solidify it in your mind.

## Step 4: Create Your Environment

It's important to avoid distractions while you study. This includes both the obvious distractions like visitors and the subtle distractions like an uncomfortable chair (or a too-comfortable couch that makes you want to fall asleep). Set up the best study environment possible: good lighting and a comfortable work area. If background music helps you focus, you may want to turn it on, but otherwise keep the room quiet. If you are using a computer to take notes, be sure you don't have any other windows open, especially applications like social media, games, or anything else that could distract you. Silence your phone and turn off notifications. Be sure to keep water close by so you stay hydrated while you study (but avoid unhealthy drinks and snacks).

Also, take into account the best time of day to study. Are you freshest first thing in the morning? Try to set aside some time then to work through the material. Is your mind clearer in the afternoon or evening? Schedule your study session then. Another method is to study at the same time of day that you will take the test, so that your brain gets used to working on the material at that time and will be ready to focus at test time.

**Step 5: Study!**

Once you have done all the study preparation, it's time to settle into the actual studying. Sit down, take a few moments to settle your mind so you can focus, and begin to follow your study plan. Don't give in to distractions or let yourself procrastinate. This is your time to prepare so you'll be ready to fearlessly approach the test. Make the most of the time and stay focused.

Of course, you don't want to burn out. If you study too long you may find that you're not retaining the information very well. Take regular study breaks. For example, taking five minutes out of every hour to walk briskly, breathing deeply and swinging your arms, can help your mind stay fresh.

As you get to the end of each chapter or section, it's a good idea to do a quick review. Remind yourself of what you learned and work on any difficult parts. When you feel that you've mastered the material, move on to the next part. At the end of your study session, briefly skim through your notes again.

But while review is helpful, cramming last minute is NOT. If at all possible, work ahead so that you won't need to fit all your study into the last day. Cramming overloads your brain with more information than it can process and retain, and your tired mind may struggle to recall even previously learned information when it is overwhelmed with last-minute study. Also, the urgent nature of cramming and the stress placed on your brain contribute to anxiety. You'll be more likely to go to the test feeling unprepared and having trouble thinking clearly.

So don't cram, and don't stay up late before the test, even just to review your notes at a leisurely pace. Your brain needs rest more than it needs to go over the information again. In fact, plan to finish your studies by noon or early afternoon the day before the test. Give your brain the rest of the day to relax or focus on other things, and get a good night's sleep. Then you will be fresh for the test and better able to recall what you've studied.

**Step 6: Take a practice test**

Many courses offer sample tests, either online or in the study materials. This is an excellent resource to check whether you have mastered the material, as well as to prepare for the test format and environment.

Check the test format ahead of time: the number of questions, the type (multiple choice, free response, etc.), and the time limit. Then create a plan for working through them. For example, if you have 30 minutes to take a 60-question test, your limit is 30 seconds per question. Spend less time on the questions you know well so that you can take more time on the difficult ones.

If you have time to take several practice tests, take the first one open book, with no time limit. Work through the questions at your own pace and make sure you fully understand them. Gradually work up to taking a test under test conditions: sit at a desk with all study materials put away and set a timer. Pace yourself to make sure you finish the test with time to spare and go back to check your answers if you have time.

After each test, check your answers. On the questions you missed, be sure you understand why you missed them. Did you misread the question (tests can use tricky wording)? Did you forget the information? Or was it something you hadn't learned? Go back and study any shaky areas that the practice tests reveal.

Taking these tests not only helps with your grade, but also aids in combating test anxiety. If you're already used to the test conditions, you're less likely to worry about it, and working through tests until you're scoring well gives you a confidence boost. Go through the practice tests until you feel comfortable, and then you can go into the test knowing that you're ready for it.

## Test Tips

On test day, you should be confident, knowing that you've prepared well and are ready to answer the questions. But aside from preparation, there are several test day strategies you can employ to maximize your performance.

First, as stated before, get a good night's sleep the night before the test (and for several nights before that, if possible). Go into the test with a fresh, alert mind rather than staying up late to study.

Try not to change too much about your normal routine on the day of the test. It's important to eat a nutritious breakfast, but if you normally don't eat breakfast at all, consider eating just a protein bar. If you're a coffee drinker, go ahead and have your normal coffee. Just make sure you time it so that the caffeine doesn't wear off right in the middle of your test. Avoid sugary beverages, and drink enough water to stay hydrated but not so much that you need a restroom break 10 minutes into the test. If your test isn't first thing in the morning, consider going for a walk or doing a light workout before the test to get your blood flowing.

Allow yourself enough time to get ready, and leave for the test with plenty of time to spare so you won't have the anxiety of scrambling to arrive in time. Another reason to be early is to select a good seat. It's helpful to sit away from doors and windows, which can be distracting. Find a good seat, get out your supplies, and settle your mind before the test begins.

When the test begins, start by going over the instructions carefully, even if you already know what to expect. Make sure you avoid any careless mistakes by following the directions.

Then begin working through the questions, pacing yourself as you've practiced. If you're not sure on an answer, don't spend too much time on it, and don't let it shake your confidence. Either skip it and come back later, or eliminate as many wrong answers as possible and guess among the remaining ones. Don't dwell on these questions as you continue—put them out of your mind and focus on what lies ahead.

Be sure to read all of the answer choices, even if you're sure the first one is the right answer. Sometimes you'll find a better one if you keep reading. But don't second-guess yourself if you do immediately know the answer. Your gut instinct is usually right. Don't let test anxiety rob you of the information you know.

If you have time at the end of the test (and if the test format allows), go back and review your answers. Be cautious about changing any, since your first instinct tends to be correct, but make sure you didn't misread any of the questions or accidentally mark the wrong answer choice. Look over any you skipped and make an educated guess.

At the end, leave the test feeling confident. You've done your best, so don't waste time worrying about your performance or wishing you could change anything. Instead, celebrate the successful completion of this test. And finally, use this test to learn how to deal with anxiety even better next time.

> **Review Video:** 5 Tips to Beat Test Anxiety
> Visit mometrix.com/academy and enter code: 570656

## Important Qualification

Not all anxiety is created equal. If your test anxiety is causing major issues in your life beyond the classroom or testing center, or if you are experiencing troubling physical symptoms related to your anxiety, it may be a sign of a serious physiological or psychological condition. If this sounds like your situation, we strongly encourage you to seek professional help.

# How to Overcome Your Fear of Math

The word *math* is enough to strike fear into most hearts. How many of us have memories of sitting through confusing lectures, wrestling over mind-numbing homework, or taking tests that still seem incomprehensible even after hours of study? Years after graduation, many still shudder at these memories.

The fact is, math is not just a classroom subject. It has real-world implications that you face every day, whether you realize it or not. This may be balancing your monthly budget, deciding how many supplies to buy for a project, or simply splitting a meal check with friends. The idea of daily confrontations with math can be so paralyzing that some develop a condition known as *math anxiety*.

But you do NOT need to be paralyzed by this anxiety! In fact, while you may have thought all your life that you're not good at math, or that your brain isn't wired to understand it, the truth is that you may have been conditioned to think this way. From your earliest school days, the way you were taught affected the way you viewed different subjects. And the way math has been taught has changed.

Several decades ago, there was a shift in American math classrooms. The focus changed from traditional problem-solving to a conceptual view of topics, de-emphasizing the importance of learning the basics and building on them. The solid foundation necessary for math progression and confidence was undermined. Math became more of a vague concept than a concrete idea. Today, it is common to think of math, not as a straightforward system, but as a mysterious, complicated method that can't be fully understood unless you're a genius.

This is why you may still have nightmares about being called on to answer a difficult problem in front of the class. Math anxiety is a very real, though unnecessary, fear.

Math anxiety may begin with a single class period. Let's say you missed a day in 6th grade math and never quite understood the concept that was taught while you were gone. Since math is cumulative, with each new concept building on past ones, this could very well affect the rest of your math career. Without that one day's knowledge, it will be difficult to understand any other concepts that link to it. Rather than realizing that you're just missing one key piece, you may begin to believe that you're simply not capable of understanding math.

This belief can change the way you approach other classes, career options, and everyday life experiences, if you become anxious at the thought that math might be required. A student who loves science may choose a different path of study upon realizing that multiple math classes will be required for a degree. An aspiring medical student may hesitate at the thought of going through the necessary math classes. For some this anxiety escalates into a more extreme state known as *math phobia*.

Math anxiety is challenging to address because it is rooted deeply and may come from a variety of causes: an embarrassing moment in class, a teacher who did not explain concepts well and contributed to a shaky foundation, or a failed test that contributed to the belief of math failure.

These causes add up over time, encouraged by society's popular view that math is hard and unpleasant. Eventually a person comes to firmly believe that he or she is simply bad at math. This belief makes it difficult to grasp new concepts or even remember old ones. Homework and test grades begin to slip, which only confirms the belief. The poor performance is not due to lack of ability but is caused by math anxiety.

Math anxiety is an emotional issue, not a lack of intelligence. But when it becomes deeply rooted, it can become more than just an emotional problem. Physical symptoms appear. Blood pressure may rise and heartbeat may quicken at the sight of a math problem – or even the thought of math! This fear leads to a mental block. When someone with math anxiety is asked to perform a calculation, even a basic problem can seem overwhelming and impossible. The emotional and physical response to the thought of math prevents the brain from working through it logically.

The more this happens, the more a person's confidence drops, and the more math anxiety is generated. This vicious cycle must be broken!

The first step in breaking the cycle is to go back to very beginning and make sure you really understand the basics of how math works and why it works. It is not enough to memorize rules for multiplication and division. If you don't know WHY these rules work, your foundation will be shaky and you will be at risk of developing a phobia. Understanding mathematical concepts not only promotes confidence and security, but allows you to build on this understanding for new concepts. Additionally, you can solve unfamiliar problems using familiar concepts and processes.

Why is it that students in other countries regularly outperform American students in math? The answer likely boils down to a couple of things: the foundation of mathematical conceptual understanding and societal perception. While students in the US are not expected to *like* or *get* math, in many other nations, students are expected not only to understand math but also to excel at it.

Changing the American view of math that leads to math anxiety is a monumental task. It requires changing the training of teachers nationwide, from kindergarten through high school, so that they learn to teach the *why* behind math and to combat the wrong math views that students may develop. It also involves changing the stigma associated with math, so that it is no longer viewed as unpleasant and incomprehensible. While these are necessary changes, they are challenging and will take time. But in the meantime, math anxiety is not irreversible—it can be faced and defeated, one person at a time.

## False Beliefs

One reason math anxiety has taken such hold is that several false beliefs have been created and shared until they became widely accepted. Some of these unhelpful beliefs include the following:

***There is only one way to solve a math problem***. In the same way that you can choose from different driving routes and still arrive at the same house, you can solve a math problem using different methods and still find the correct answer. A person who understands the reasoning behind math calculations may be able to look at an unfamiliar concept and find the right answer, just by applying logic to the knowledge they already have. This approach may be different than what is taught in the classroom, but it is still valid. Unfortunately, even many teachers view math as a subject where the best course of action is to memorize the rule or process for each problem rather than as a place for students to exercise logic and creativity in finding a solution.

***Many people don't have a mind for math***. A person who has struggled due to poor teaching or math anxiety may falsely believe that he or she doesn't have the mental capacity to grasp mathematical concepts. Most of the time, this is false. Many people find that when they are relieved of their math anxiety, they have more than enough brainpower to understand math.

***Men are naturally better at math than women***. Even though research has shown this to be false, many young women still avoid math careers and classes because of their belief that their math abilities are inferior. Many girls have come to believe that math is a male skill and have given up trying to understand or enjoy it.

***Counting aids are bad***. Something like counting on your fingers or drawing out a problem to visualize it may be frowned on as childish or a crutch, but these devices can help you get a tangible understanding of a problem or a concept.

Sadly, many students buy into these ideologies at an early age. A young girl who enjoys math class may be conditioned to think that she doesn't actually have the brain for it because math is for boys, and may turn her energies to other pursuits, permanently closing the door on a wide range of opportunities. A child who finds the right answer but doesn't follow the teacher's method may believe that he is doing it wrong and isn't good at math. A student who never had a problem with math before may have a poor teacher and become confused, yet believe that the problem is because she doesn't have a mathematical mind.

Students who have bought into these erroneous beliefs quickly begin to add their own anxieties, adapting them to their own personal situations:

***I'll never use this in real life***. A huge number of people wrongly believe that math is irrelevant outside the classroom. By adopting this mindset, they are handicapping themselves for a life in a mathematical world, as well as limiting their career choices. When they are inevitably faced with real-world math, they are conditioning themselves to respond with anxiety.

***I'm not quick enough***. While timed tests and quizzes, or even simply comparing yourself with other students in the class, can lead to this belief, speed is not an indicator of skill level. A person can work very slowly yet understand at a deep level.

***If I can understand it, it's too easy***. People with a low view of their own abilities tend to think that if they are able to grasp a concept, it must be simple. They cannot accept the idea that they are capable of understanding math. This belief will make it harder to learn, no matter how intelligent they are.

***I just can't learn this***. An overwhelming number of people think this, from young children to adults, and much of the time it is simply not true. But this mindset can turn into a self-fulfilling prophecy that keeps you from exercising and growing your math ability.

The good news is, each of these myths can be debunked. For most people, they are based on emotion and psychology, NOT on actual ability! It will take time, effort, and the desire to change, but change is possible. Even if you have spent years thinking that you don't have the capability to understand math, it is not too late to uncover your true ability and find relief from the anxiety that surrounds math.

# Math Strategies

It is important to have a plan of attack to combat math anxiety. There are many useful strategies for pinpointing the fears or myths and eradicating them:

***Go back to the basics***. For most people, math anxiety stems from a poor foundation. You may think that you have a complete understanding of addition and subtraction, or even decimals and percentages, but make absolutely sure. Learning math is different from learning other subjects. For example, when you learn history, you study various time periods and places and events. It may be important to memorize dates or find out about the lives of famous people. When you move from US history to world history, there will be some overlap, but a large amount of the information will be new. Mathematical concepts, on the other hand, are very closely linked and highly dependent on each other. It's like climbing a ladder – if a rung is missing from your understanding, it may be difficult or impossible for you to climb any higher, no matter how hard you try. So go back and make sure your math foundation is strong. This may mean taking a remedial math course, going to a tutor to work through the shaky concepts, or just going through your old homework to make sure you really understand it.

***Speak the language***. Math has a large vocabulary of terms and phrases unique to working problems. Sometimes these are completely new terms, and sometimes they are common words, but are used differently in a math setting. If you can't speak the language, it will be very difficult to get a thorough understanding of the concepts. It's common for students to think that they don't understand math when they simply don't understand the vocabulary. The good news is that this is fairly easy to fix. Brushing up on any terms you aren't quite sure of can help bring the rest of the concepts into focus.

***Check your anxiety level***. When you think about math, do you feel nervous or uncomfortable? Do you struggle with feelings of inadequacy, even on concepts that you know you've already learned? It's important to understand your specific math anxieties, and what triggers them. When you catch yourself falling back on a false belief, mentally replace it with the truth. Don't let yourself believe that you can't learn, or that struggling with a concept means you'll never understand it. Instead, remind yourself of how much you've already learned and dwell on that past success. Visualize grasping the new concept, linking it to your old knowledge, and moving on to the next challenge. Also, learn how to manage anxiety when it arises. There are many techniques for coping with the irrational fears that rise to the surface when you enter the math classroom. This may include controlled breathing, replacing negative thoughts with positive ones, or visualizing success. Anxiety interferes with your ability to concentrate and absorb information, which in turn contributes to greater anxiety. If you can learn how to regain control of your thinking, you will be better able to pay attention, make progress, and succeed!

***Don't go it alone***. Like any deeply ingrained belief, math anxiety is not easy to eradicate. And there is no need for you to wrestle through it on your own. It will take time, and many people find that speaking with a counselor or psychiatrist helps. They can help you develop strategies for responding to anxiety and overcoming old ideas. Additionally, it can be very helpful to take a short course or seek out a math tutor to help you find and fix the missing rungs on your ladder and make sure that you're ready to progress to the next level. You can also find a number of math aids online: courses that will teach you mental devices for figuring out problems, how to get the most out of your math classes, etc.

***Check your math attitude***. No matter how much you want to learn and overcome your anxiety, you'll have trouble if you still have a negative attitude toward math. If you think it's too hard, or just have general feelings of dread about math, it will be hard to learn and to break through the anxiety. Work on cultivating a positive math attitude. Remind yourself that math is not just a hurdle to be cleared, but a valuable asset. When you view math with a positive attitude, you'll be much more likely to understand and even enjoy it. This is something you must do for yourself. You may find it helpful to visit with a counselor. Your tutor, friends, and family may cheer you on in your endeavors. But your greatest asset is yourself. You are inside your own mind – tell yourself what you need to hear. Relive past victories. Remind yourself that you are capable of understanding math. Root out any false beliefs that linger and replace them with positive truths. Even if it doesn't feel true at first, it will begin to affect your thinking and pave the way for a positive, anxiety-free mindset.

Aside from these general strategies, there are a number of specific practical things you can do to begin your journey toward overcoming math anxiety. Something as simple as learning a new note-taking strategy can change the way you approach math and give you more confidence and understanding. New study techniques can also make a huge difference.

Math anxiety leads to bad habits. If it causes you to be afraid of answering a question in class, you may gravitate toward the back row. You may be embarrassed to ask for help. And you may procrastinate on assignments, which leads to rushing through them at the last moment when it's too late to get a better understanding. It's important to identify your negative behaviors and replace them with positive ones:

*Prepare ahead of time*. Read the lesson before you go to class. Being exposed to the topics that will be covered in class ahead of time, even if you don't understand them perfectly, is extremely helpful in increasing what you retain from the lecture. Do your homework and, if you're still shaky, go over some extra problems. The key to a solid understanding of math is practice.

*Sit front and center*. When you can easily see and hear, you'll understand more, and you'll avoid the distractions of other students if no one is in front of you. Plus, you're more likely to be sitting with students who are positive and engaged, rather than others with math anxiety. Let their positive math attitude rub off on you.

*Ask questions in class and out*. If you don't understand something, just ask. If you need a more in-depth explanation, the teacher may need to work with you outside of class, but often it's a simple concept you don't quite understand, and a single question may clear it up. If you wait, you may not be able to follow the rest of the day's lesson. For extra help, most professors have office hours outside of class when you can go over concepts one-on-one to clear up any uncertainties. Additionally, there may be a *math lab* or study session you can attend for homework help. Take advantage of this.

*Review*. Even if you feel that you've fully mastered a concept, review it periodically to reinforce it. Going over an old lesson has several benefits: solidifying your understanding, giving you a confidence boost, and even giving some new insights into material that you're currently learning! Don't let yourself get rusty. That can lead to problems with learning later concepts.

# Teaching Tips

While the math student's mindset is the most crucial to overcoming math anxiety, it is also important for others to adjust their math attitudes. Teachers and parents have an enormous influence on how students relate to math. They can either contribute to math confidence or math anxiety.

As a parent or teacher, it is very important to convey a positive math attitude. Retelling horror stories of your own bad experience with math will contribute to a new generation of math anxiety. Even if you don't share your experiences, others will be able to sense your fears and may begin to believe them.

Even a careless comment can have a big impact, so watch for phrases like *He's not good at math* or *I never liked math*. You are a crucial role model, and your children or students will unconsciously adopt your mindset. Give them a positive example to follow. Rather than teaching them to fear the math world before they even know it, teach them about all its potential and excitement.

Work to present math as an integral, beautiful, and understandable part of life. Encourage creativity in solving problems. Watch for false beliefs and dispel them. Cross the lines between subjects: integrate history, English, and music with math. Show students how math is used every day, and how the entire world is based on mathematical principles, from the pull of gravity to the shape of seashells. Instead of letting students see math as a necessary evil, direct them to view it as an imaginative, beautiful art form – an art form that they are capable of mastering and using.

Don't give too narrow a view of math. It is more than just numbers. Yes, working problems and learning formulas is a large part of classroom math. But don't let the teaching stop there. Teach students about the everyday implications of math. Show them how nature works according to the laws of mathematics, and take them outside to make discoveries of their own. Expose them to math-related careers by inviting visiting speakers, asking students to do research and presentations, and learning students' interests and aptitudes on a personal level.

Demonstrate the importance of math. Many people see math as nothing more than a required stepping stone to their degree, a nuisance with no real usefulness. Teach students that algebra is used every day in managing their bank accounts, in following recipes, and in scheduling the day's events. Show them how learning to do geometric proofs helps them to develop logical thinking, an invaluable life skill. Let them see that math surrounds them and is integrally linked to their daily lives: that weather predictions are based on math, that math was used to design cars and other machines, etc. Most of all, give them the tools to use math to enrich their lives.

Make math as tangible as possible. Use visual aids and objects that can be touched. It is much easier to grasp a concept when you can hold it in your hands and manipulate it, rather than just listening to the lecture. Encourage math outside of the classroom. The real world is full of measuring, counting, and calculating, so let students participate in this. Keep your eyes open for numbers and patterns to discuss. Talk about how scores are calculated in sports games and how far apart plants are placed in a garden row for maximum growth. Build the mindset that math is a normal and interesting part of daily life.

Finally, find math resources that help to build a positive math attitude. There are a number of books that show math as fascinating and exciting while teaching important concepts, for example: *The Math Curse; A Wrinkle in Time; The Phantom Tollbooth;* and *Fractals, Googols and Other Mathematical Tales*. You can also find a number of online resources: math puzzles and games, videos that show math in nature, and communities of math enthusiasts. On a local level, students can compete in a variety of math competitions with other schools or join a math club.

The student who experiences math as exciting and interesting is unlikely to suffer from math anxiety. Going through life without this handicap is an immense advantage and opens many doors that others have closed through their fear.

## Self-Check

Whether you suffer from math anxiety or not, chances are that you have been exposed to some of the false beliefs mentioned above. Now is the time to check yourself for any errors you may have accepted. Do you think you're not wired for math? Or that you don't need to understand it since you're not planning on a math career? Do you think math is just too difficult for the average person?

Find the errors you've taken to heart and replace them with positive thinking. Are you capable of learning math? Yes! Can you control your anxiety? Yes! These errors will resurface from time to time, so be watchful. Don't let others with math anxiety influence you or sway your confidence. If you're having trouble with a concept, find help. Don't let it discourage you!

Create a plan of attack for defeating math anxiety and sharpening your skills. Do some research and decide if it would help you to take a class, get a tutor, or find some online resources to fine-tune your knowledge. Make the effort to get good nutrition, hydration, and sleep so that you are operating at full capacity. Remind yourself daily that you are skilled and that anxiety does not control you. Your mind is capable of so much more than you know. Give it the tools it needs to grow and thrive.

# Thank You

We at Mometrix would like to extend our heartfelt thanks to you, our friend and patron, for allowing us to play a part in your journey. It is a privilege to serve people from all walks of life who are unified in their commitment to building the best future they can for themselves.

The preparation you devote to these important testing milestones may be the most valuable educational opportunity you have for making a real difference in your life. We encourage you to put your heart into it—that feeling of succeeding, overcoming, and yes, conquering will be well worth the hours you've invested.

We want to hear your story, your struggles and your successes, and if you see any opportunities for us to improve our materials so we can help others even more effectively in the future, please share that with us as well. **The team at Mometrix would be absolutely thrilled to hear from you!** So please, send us an email (support@mometrix.com) and let's stay in touch.

If you'd like some additional help, check out these other resources we offer for your exam:

http://MometrixFlashcards.com/STAAR

# Additional Bonus Material

Due to our efforts to try to keep this book to a manageable length, we've created a link that will give you access to all of your additional bonus material.

Please visit https://www.mometrix.com/bonus948/staarg6math to access the information.